Wine: Both Barrels
Olly Smith's World of Wine

Olly Smith

"Lots of love from Isabel + Imogen"

CHEERS!

First published in Great Britain in 2012
by Hot Bottle Press, Lewes BN7 1YJ

The right of Olly Smith to be identified as Author
of this Work has been asserted by him in accordance
with the Copyright, Designs and Patents Act 1988

www.ollysmith.com

A CIP catalogue for this book is available from the British Library

ISBN 978 0 9574480 0 1

Designed by Cosima Dinkel
Front Cover photography by Alun Callender
Printed and bound in the United Kingdom by CPI Anthony Rowe

Wine: Both Barrels
Olly Smith's World of Wine

Olly Smith

Read more from Olly every week in *Live*, catch Olly online and sign up for Hot Bottle, his free wine email bulletin at www.ollysmith.com, join the wine chat on his Facebook fan page, follow him on Twitter @jollyolly and learn about wine through his Wine App (imaginatively called 'Olly Smith's Wine App') which delivers all Olly's wine knowledge direct to your fingertips.

Thanks to...
Andrew Davies, Gerard Greaves and Geordie Grieg at
the *Mail on Sunday*; The team at *Live Magazine*; My family.

Sub-Editor Richard Hemming for subbing magnificently.

Cosima Dinkel for designing this book so beautifully.

Jess Hood for compiling these columns.

Alun Callender for snapping the cover photo.

Thanks, praise, hugs and adorings to my amazing wife
Sophie for such tremendous support in everything.

Contents

Barolo, Puligny, Sancerre...
without the price tag (if you know how)

Why is it that George Clooney scoops all the mega roles when supposedly lesser actors struggle to get a bit part? Is he really a finer actor? Is his stubble truly more rugged than the rest? Clearly his name counts for a lot.

Yet when I go to the cinema, I pay the same price for a ticket whether he's in the movie or not. With wine we're led to believe that the good stuff will be pricey and the bad stuff cheap. But that's not the whole story.

The value of wine is a mystic equation that would send Einstein's brain into a spin. Part of it is covered by production costs – equipment, barrels, land, packaging, transport, storage and selling.

But you've also got the elusive star factor: is this booze iconic, unique, special, and how many people want a splash of it? Is it George Clooney? Or just some stubbly bloke called George? Wine sellers, it seems, are far cannier than the movie producers, as they've made a fortune by charging far more for the George Clooneys of the grape world.

Think about the famous names in wine – Chablis, Bordeaux, Barolo... what do they actually mean to you? A lot of the time, the name tells you very little about the wine – it might be the name of a village or a region rather than the grape or quality of the liquid.

Alongside price, the really key information is what flavours to expect, who made it, what year it is and whether it goes well with the meal you're having. Frankly, you can forget everything else.

Take Sancerre. It's named after a French village in the Loire famous for producing white wine with pinging, super-fresh verve. It tastes a bit like a grapefruit plugged into the mains. The grape is Sauvignon Blanc. Now, if you're a fan of Sancerre but want to save a few pounds, grab a Sauvignon de Touraine from just down the road – a deft and glorious white wine poised between the Loire and Marlborough, and much less expensive than Sancerre.Or try Sauvignon Blanc from places such as South Africa (Elgin), Chile (Leyda) or New Zealand (Marlborough). Each of these regions produces a unique style but each is linked by a zesty, joyful, upbeat freshness that's capable of making Monday feel more like Friday.

Drinking top-end wine can be a minefield but there are ways to treat your taste buds without having to hawk the family jewels. The supermarket shelves are littered with bargains if you know where to look – and how to look for them. Sometimes famous wines have neighbouring vineyards that offer similar quality at a snip of the price. For example, if you're a fan of pricey Puligny-Montrachet try the neighbouring vineyards of St-Aubin for a brilliant bargain.

A producer worth looking out for is Domaine Gérard Thomas – who makes complex, world class white wine with real polish and finesse. However, there's even more value to be had by looking for a talented winemaking region producing the same grape even further afield. In the case of Puligny and St-Aubin, we're talking Chardonnay with a touch of oak. And a beautiful region in France to look at for astounding class and value in Chardonnay is Limoux.

If you consider skipping the big brand names and going for smaller local producers to keep costs down, your wallet may grin at you. And don't be scared to try supermarket own-label booze either.

A lot of these wines are made by the same winemakers as the pricier stuff – and remember, it's always what's in the bottle that counts.

War of the rosés

Rosé used to be a little like Clark Kent. Bumbling, a bit wimpy and thought of by blokes as a wishy-washy wine that couldn't make up its mind if it were white or red.

Yet today rosé is one of the most rapidly growing wine categories – it's a mainstream drink that works with a wide range of dishes and is arguably the best accompaniment to a summery afternoon.

Unlike a lot of red wine, rosé feels instantly informal, accessible and familiar. In years gone by, men would happily sip a glass of pink on holiday in Provence, but as soon as our feet hit Blighty, chilled pink was strictly for girls.

And yet, when you think about rosé champagne, it's been a drink of class, prestige and an acceptably flashy purchase for years. Don't be deceived by its Clark Kent demeanour: rosé can be full of surprises.

Firstly, there is no such thing as simple rosé any more. There are a myriad of different styles to choose from – from very pale offerings to neon pink, and even rosé that is so dark and butch it's practically red.

There are some big brand names from California that produce commercial styles of rosé which I find too sweet – but there's no denying their popularity.

It's easy to find bottles from all over the world and from lots of different grape varieties – Shiraz, Cabernet Sauvignon, Pinot Noir and many others. You can hunt down crisp styles from Provence, elegantly fruity styles from Rioja, fruit bombs from just about anywhere – and even some famous names such as Sancerre rosé made from the elfin Pinot Noir grape.

The best news is that where rosé is concerned, in general your wallet is not going to get a pummelling – unless you buy champagne, where some of the prestige rosés can fetch upwards of £150.

Rosé is generally made to drink right away – you can lay down prestigious examples but if you ask me, rosé is all about fresh fruit. It's the wine equivalent to the first strawberry of the season and the sun beating down as you give in to the irresistible urge to do absolutely nothing.

And you know exactly when to drink it – immediately.

Does a medal on a bottle mean it's delicious?

How can a wine possibly win an award?

It's not like a bottle of vino is capable of running 100 metres.

Well, I'm a senior judge for the International Wine Challenge, The Decanter World Wine Awards and a host of other boozy contests, and these events are a bit like the Olympics of wine – partly because the tasting sessions can be marathons of endurance, but also because wines are divided into heats.

The key thing to look for is a sense of balance and proportion. Think of it like a Formula One racing car: you want four elements to be in balance, like the four tyres on the track.

The four things to balance in wine are alcohol, tannins, acidity and body. In the middle of these the flavours are held together, a bit like the engine.

The more complex the flavours, the finer the wine. An overall sense of harmony between all these elements is what you're after.

So is it worth hunting for an award-winner?

Choosing a gold (or silver, or bronze) is a useful way of tasting something new, safe in the knowledge that it's of a certain quality.

The selection process for these awards is rigorous – each wine is evaluated by a panel of wine professionals chaired by a senior member of the trade: a Jedi Knight of wine. The first phase is to weed out the dead wood.

The next step is to establish whether the wine is worthy of a bronze, silver or gold medal. If it strikes gold, the panel has to decide whether the wine is good enough to go forward for a further trophy such as 'Best Red Under £10'. The great thing about awards is they can throw the spotlight onto rising quality from smaller regions.

You may find a difference between wines winning awards in different parts of the world. In the US, judges have a reputation for singling out wines with full-on flavour for glory, whereas Europeans tend to prize lower alcohol and elegance more highly.

The three big UK wine awards to look out for are the International Wine Challenge, the Decanter World Wine Awards and the International Wine and Spirit Competition.

Going for gold is a handy benchmark when buying wine, but ultimately what matters is whether you find yourself cheering after the first sip. On your marks, get set... cheers!

Bottles for the barbie

The coals are warming, the sun is piping hot and there's only an hour before the charcoal has burned to the optimum ash white for sizzling those steaks.

That leaves plenty of time to think hard about drinking well. My top tip for barbecue wines is to divide the day into three distinct zones: the pre-feasting, the gorging zone and the sated hammock-induced snooze.

To begin with, you want light, crisp wines that'll make your guests giggle and improve your chances of a summery cuddle further down the track. New Zealand Sauvignon Blanc, Albariño from Galicia in Spain, crisp pale rosé, Aussie dry Riesling and South African Chenin Blanc are all top choices.

If it's fizz you're after, I prefer sipping something simple and good value such as Italian Prosecco. You could stretch your Prosecco further and add a delicious dollop of peach purée to the bottom of each glass to make easy Bellinis.

That said, it's super-simple to whip up a purée yourself – peel some peaches, chop and remove the stones, blitz in a blender (add sugar if you must) and there you have it.

Another top tip I learned while in Chile is to chop fresh strawberries into a jug of ice-cold white wine. A simple fruit punch.

When the snacks are about to be served, move on to fruity red wines. And here's a big tip – I love to serve red wine chilled with a barbecue.

Don't bother chilling any serious old vintage wine or any big hefty reds – experiment with grape varieties such as Pinot Noir, Malbec, Cabernet Franc, Grenache, Carignan and Nero d'Avola.

Chilling red wine tends to bring out fruit flavours, and on a hot day it'll last longer in the glass before it heats up like a simmering cauldron in your hand. Plus the wine feels more refreshing alongside a juicy burger – and chilled reds can even work with meaty fish such as tuna or swordfish steaks.

Once the barbecue is done, you can freestyle as you dive into your deckchair, but if you fancy something cold and sweet to round off your alfresco feast, you can't go wrong with a dessert wine – known as 'stickies' in the trade – such as Muscat served in short tumblers over crushed ice.

In this case, the crushed ice lifts the drink and it becomes a dessert in its own right. Cheers!

Go with the low: perfect wines with little alcohol content

There's been a fad recently for wines with reduced alcohol. I have yet to taste one that puts a spring in my step.

Instead I get a creeping sense of meanness, of being cheated, that the thing in my glass is a bit like steak minus meat, champagne *sans bubbles,* Lewis Hamilton without winning. It's flat, forgettable and enough to curdle my mayonnaise.

The great news is that there are plenty of wines that are naturally low in alcohol and absolutely perfect for a lunchtime drop or to grace your picnic hamper.

Hot climates tend to produce wines with a higher alcohol content, as more natural sugar is accumulated in the grapes thanks to the roasting sun.

So in general, if you're after lower alcohol, look to cooler climates – for example English wine, French Loire wines, cool coastal wines as exemplified by many New Zealand regions, wines near Antarctica, as in the case of Tasmania, wines beside rivers, such as German Rieslings, or wines from very high up, as in the case of several Argentinian Malbecs, which are grown so high up in the Andes that you'd need a spaceship to visit the vineyards.

Anything that lowers the temperature in the vineyard will help to reduce the sugar content. But man can also intervene to arrest the level of alcohol during fermentation, either by chilling the fermentation down to kill the yeast, or by filtering the yeast out.

A good example is Asti Spumante – generally around 7.5 per cent alcohol. Genius.

Others you could investigate include German reds, white wines from the tiny Basque region of Txakoli/Chacoli, which are delightfully crisp with a spritz and generally between 9.5 and 11.5 per cent alcohol, or peer back through time at the oft-forgotten realm of Muscadet.

The best of these are generally Muscadet-Sur-Lie, meaning they've had more time on the dead yeast cells, which imparts a touch of savoury complexity.

Serve highly chilled for a simple accompaniment to your lunchtime mussels.

And if you're really keen to bring down the alcohol in your vino, toss in some freshly chopped fruit and a few glugs of lemonade and bingo, you have a convenient low-alcohol fruit punch. Cheers!

Supermarket own-label wines deserve a fitting tribute

Bon Giovi down the local pub are never quite going to blow your mind with the stadium-filling coiffured power of Bon Jovi, but tribute bands are a growing phenomenon.

In Chile on a recent wine tasting tour, I witnessed the Beatles playing at a downtown Santiago bar – so good it was almost impossible to tell the difference from the real thing.

Is it the same with wine? Can supermarket own-label vino touch the giddy heights of the branded stuff?

Of course it can.

For starters, own-label wines are frequently made by the same winemaker at exactly the same winery as the more famous brands. What's more, own-label wines often pick up some impressive awards. They're all at it: whichever supermarket you frequent, there is bound to be an impressive selection of their own wine proudly on display.

If you're still too ashamed to show a supermarket label in front of guests, a white napkin wrapped around a bottle always makes wine look pricier than it is – and when your guests sip it, you'll look like the king of good taste.

Avoiding the guilty morning after:
the ethical approach to buying wine

I once worked alongside Hugh Fearnley-Whittingstall at the Taste of London festival, and I'll admit that as well as being a pal, Hugh is one of my heroes.

His inspiring approach to food has unmasked a world of shameless murk in our food production. But how about wine? What horrors lurk behind the scenes from vineyard to glass? Are there ways to buy wines more ethically?

Well, yes, is the short answer – you just need to ask yourself what you're most concerned about. If it's simply finding the finest wine at the cheapest price, you can start by avoiding 'buy one, get one free' offers. BOGOFs may be tempting, but where wine is concerned they rarely offer real value – the wine is almost certainly listed at an inflated price to begin with.

You can treat your wallet and your palate better by sourcing wine that's fairly priced and encourages winemakers to focus on quality.

If your carbon footprint keeps you awake at night, shun bottles which require the biceps of Arnie to lift and a billion litres of oil to ship to your tongue. Heavy bottles are ludicrous, and I'm delighted that more and more producers are looking to switch to lighter bottles.

You can even buy plastic bottles of wine that bounce if they fall on the floor – although for me they seem to impart an icky flavour to the booze. That said, it's certainly an area to watch.

Meanwhile, if you're keen to reduce the impact of pesticides and herbicides, buy organic, *lutte raisonné* (nearly organic) or, best of all, biodynamic wines – whose makers treat the entire vineyard with the respect of a living organism. It's debatable whether flavour is improved via biodynamics, but it does encourage close attention to detail. You could try seeking out organic and biodynamic wines from online specialists.

Perhaps your biggest worry is whether the workers are getting a fair deal, in which case Fairtrade is a label to hunt – I've seen Fairtrade wineries in operation, and their social benefit is tangible.

That said, Fairtrade wine ought to be of excellent quality as well as socially responsible, and cost a bit more if the quality merits it. Which brings me to my final point on the ethics of wine: whatever the price, never serve a wine to your guests that you wouldn't happily sip for the rest of your life.

Pop these with your poppadom: which wine to go with your curry

You might think that wine with a curry is the food equivalent of eating a meteorite – exotic and flashy but ultimately pointless.

I've never eaten a meteorite, but to be honest I'd quite fancy giving one a lick if it tumbled into my back yard; you just never know where the next taste sensation might come from.

With curry and wine, there's a massive difference between ordering a Ruby Murray from the local curry house and tasting Michelin-starred Indian cuisine.

Britain now boasts some truly world class ambassadors of Indian excellence, who work tirelessly to produce cooking that will blow your mind with its complexity, but not blow your palate with explosive spices. Their cooking majors on aromatics and fragrance, but the real secret is the depth of flavour they manage to conjure. And that makes matching wine to their cooking a real art – and one that makes my mouth water like the river Ganges.

There are about a billion different bottles to choose from. Traditionally we'd just stick a Gewürztraminer on the table with its lychee and Turkish delight-type flavours and hope or the best.

But have you tried Pinot Gris?

With such a massive range of flavours on offer across the world of vino, you'd be amazed at how well more classic wines pair up. One of the world's leading specialists in the field of matching wine with Indian food is Costanzo Scala.

'The most important thing is the level of heat and spicing in the sauce and the cooking method. A fresh, grassy Sauvignon Blanc is best with a sauce that has a sharp edge like ginger and coriander, while tandoori dishes work very well with oaky wines, which are toasty.'

In general, my tip is to avoid chunky reds. Whites with a bit of richness and oak can work sublimely with creamy dishes and sometimes fruity reds or whites can help combat spice.

One trick I love is to chill down a fruity red and enjoy it with more meaty dishes. There are even some quality wines emerging from India, such as Sula Vineyards near Mumbai, which I would love to see more of in local curry houses.

Until then, drink plenty of whatever makes you happy! Even if it happens to be essence of meteorite.

In a league of their own: which country tops the wine export charts?

Wine drinking may not be a competitive sport but the rivalry between countries to see who leads the world with the most influential palate, which wineries are leading their region, and which supermarket's buying team is ruling the roost is just as intense.

Perhaps the most brutal way to examine the world of wine is by country.

The French were once the undisputed masters of the art, but in 2009 their wine exports to the UK slid from second to third position, with the US in second and Italy in fourth.

For the nation that regards itself as the birthplace of wine, this is a royal spanking. France has amazing prestige in Champagne, Bordeaux and Burgundy, wondrous diversity in the Loire, awesomeness in the Rhône, aromatics in Alsace and some serious value emerging in the Vin de Pays / IGP category. But the French system of labelling by place rather than grape still leaves a lot of UK wine fans bewildered.

Australia has its strengths, but my tips to watch out for include New Zealand, Chile and South Africa.

Argentina, too, is worth watching: it might be lower in the league, but there's a lot of potential there. It's not just about Malbec – have you sipped Torrontés lately?And keep your eye on Spain, which is rapidly modernising with seriously sexy, innovative wines such as Albariño from Galicia – genius, like Chablis with a subtle aromatic twist.

Germany is another country with world class wine. You can buy wine from one of their most prestigious vineyards for a fraction of the price of a top French Bordeaux. Then again, you could support England's emerging bid as a wine producing nation with a bottle of crisp, summery Bacchus. Pinging white wine wreathed in the glory of British hedgerow flavours.

If we drink enough of it in years to come, you never know, we might even make the number one spot.

Drink like a chef when it comes to that top drop

Chefs generally have amazing palates, which means that even if wine isn't their speciality, they can still pick out a howler or a top vintage in seconds.

I remember once, Raymond Blanc and I were tasting wine, and – without even glancing at the bottle – he smelt a red and correctly identified a grape that formed only ten per cent of the blend. Supernose! When chefs love wine and work with their sommelier to produce perfectly tailored wine and food combinations, something magical occurs and the whole tasting experience can reach new places, revealing hidden dimensions.

One chef who really knows her vino is Angela Hartnett.

'I love wine – mainly Italian,' she says. 'I'm very pro-Italy, as I feel you can buy better cheap Italian wine than French. I especially enjoy Italian whites, which seem uniquely fruity, crisp and dry, and I'm a fan of Barolo and Barbaresco. In warm weather, pink Prosecco is fabulous. It makes us feel like the summer is really here.'

Another top wine loving cook is James Martin. James has the task of judging my wine choices on *Saturday Kitchen* – but what does he himself choose to sample?

'Well, I hate rosé!' he says.

'But I enjoy champagne, or a cool glass of white wine like Montrachet from Burgundy'.

'As far as red goes, I'm a massive fan of Italian Barolo. They cost anywhere from £20 right up to £1,000 – so make sure you get the one right for you.

'The best bottle I ever had was on the Amalfi coast at a restaurant where they reckon they have the only wine list in Italy blessed by the Pope – and there are no prices next to the wines! Pop down to the cellar and you might end up remortgaging your house.'

Flying the flag for Britain, meanwhile, are the Hairy Bikers, who fuelled their ride around the UK for a BBC television series with fabulous home-grown wine.

'English fizz is brilliant. It's been the toast of friends' dinner parties ever since.'

The grapes are the same varieties used to make champagne in France (Pinot Noir, Pinot Meunier and Chardonnay), grown in a remarkably similar soil and climate.

So, if you're ever in doubt when hunting for a top drop, do your taste buds a favour: drink like a chef.

Cheers for a fiver: how to find value for wine on a budget

Buying wine under a fiver is fraught with risk.

At that price you're only spending around 50p on actual wine. The other £4.50 goes on tax, VAT, packaging, freight, marketing and a billion other invisible skims. So under a fiver is not necessarily the sweet spot for getting the best value out of your bottle. If you pay even £1 more, you'll find the amount you're proportionally spending on the wine ramps up significantly.

However, there are still some interesting bargains to be had hovering around the £5 mark.

Chile is a country I consistently rate for value and quality. Look out for high-class Syrah from coastal San Antonio and Elqui Valley high in the Andes, good value Pinot Noir from cool southerly Bío-Bío, and crisp Sauvignon Blanc from ocean infused Leyda.

You can also find some value from Argentina in red blends and white Torrontés, but for me the real glory of Argentina kicks in at higher price points.

Sicily is packed with possibilities for quality bargains. Fiano and Grillo are grape varieties producing crisp inexpensive whites that are a billion times more interesting than Pinot Grigio. Nero d'Avola is their signature red, light-ish in body but full of juicy fruit flavour – and a good one to serve chilled.

There are also several examples of Nero d'Avola being blended to offer more interesting flavour.

Certain regions of Spain are also worth investigating: Campo de Borja, Cariñena and Castilla-La Mancha have great value wines. In general European countries can do volume and generally keep an eye on quality.

Bargain hunting is made increasingly difficult depending on the exchange rate of the Euro. But France nearly always has some good value wines to offer in the Vin de Pays / IGP category.

I'm an increasing fan of Syrah from South Africa. On a recent trip there, I also found a couple of super-elegant examples of Pinotage.

Finally, a great tip is to look at regions that have gone out of fashion. When was the last time you tasted Frascati?

Or why, at a time when Pinot Grigio rules the roost, are more people not revelling in the inexpensive delights of crisp tangy Muscadet? Because it's so eighties?

Wrong. It's so now. Drinking unfashionably has never tasted so good.

Great white wines for autumn

At that time of year when the leaves are turning gold, there's a nip in the air, you're tempted to dust off a scarf and go for a bracing stroll, but there's still the odd warm day offering a chance for a spot of late summer basking – what do you drink?

Spicy reds will be perfect with the first frosts, but they can still feel too heavy in autumn, so my tip is to get stuck into some rich whites.

The wines of Alsace would be a good starting point. They're often richly textured and go well with complex aromatic dishes such as Thai cooking. Gewürztraminer, for example, is unmistakably flamboyant, perfumed and rich.But if those aromatics are a bit too heady and intense for you, Alsace also delivers Pinot Gris, the same grape as Pinot Grigio but with more richness, flavour and personality. And you could even grab a few bottles of Alsatian Riesling for a fruity autumn windfall moment.

Further south, the Rhône has grape varieties such as Marsanne and Roussanne that can produce rich whites. One of its appellations, Condrieu, offers white wines made from Viognier that smell and taste a bit like apricots – and which sometimes offer better value than certain other famous French names.

For superb value Viognier, check out Chile; meanwhile, Torrontés from Argentina is another grape variety that has floral power and sensual aromatics. South African Semillon is sublime when elegantly aged in oak barrels, and if left in the bottle for a few years can develop an outrageously lush honeyed character.

Chardonnay, in spite of the rumours, is still very popular here in the UK. In the past we've suffered from a few too many richly oaked and cheap examples, but times have changed, and these days winemakers are much more sensitive when deploying oak in their blends. Burgundy is the most famous Chardonnay producing region, home to wines such as Meursault, Puligny and Montrachet.

Alternatively, Limoux offers terrific value Chardonnay with a deft sprinkling of oak complexity. Another area to consider is South America; some wineries in Argentina are producing world class creations.

There are lots of great whites out there with a bit more swagger and booty than the zingy varieties of which we're so enamoured. So what are you waiting for?

Go ahead and toast the turning of the leaves.

Many happy returns: wines back in fashion

The cruelty of fashion knows no bounds, and it has stomped all over various corners of the wine world. But it's high time you sampled some varieties that have fallen out of favour.

Let's start with Muscadet. Didn't we used to revel in the value and crisp simplicity of its unbridled loveliness?

It vanished along with Frankie Goes To Hollywood – but now Muscadet has been transformed thanks to modern winemaking techniques.

Better still, it's inexpensive and is amazing with a bowl of mussels. My tip?

Look for Muscadet-Sur-Lie, which tends to be of better quality and offers more bang for your buck.

And what about Frascati?

My Grandpa loved this Italian white, which used to be in every pizza place in Britain. Today you're lucky if you spot a lone bottle weeping to itself on the supermarket shelves.

It's not just regions that get tainted by the fashion of the day; entire countries can suffer. Austrian wine was damaged by the anti-freeze scandal of the Eighties. Now it's worth investigating, thanks to the grape variety Grüner Veltliner. Think of it as butch Sauvignon Blanc with rounder edges.

Perhaps even worse than an entire country falling out of fashion is the shunning of a grape variety. Gewürztraminer is often dismissed as OTT with its heady floral and sweet flavours, but it's definitely worth a try.

Finally, Chardonnay has also been kicked for pairing so well with oak. Oaky Chardonnay shouldn't curdle your mayonnaise; it's a perfectly respectable combination, only to be shunned when there's an overdose of oak in it.

And remember, with unfashionable wines you'll not only save a few quid, but also help resurrect some quality drinks. It's a win-win.

The Brits are coming: why it's time to shout about English wine

British booze is brilliant, isn't it?

You can tantalise your tongue with everything from fruity, hoppy Sussex bitter to tangy, tongue-spanking Cornish beers.

British cider and perry are both enjoying a long overdue renaissance. Whisky is wonderful. Gin is genius. But what do you really think of home-grown wine? Silence.

Well, it's time we shouted about English wines, as there are truly some belters worthy of your love and respect. I have yet to taste a red wine that really hits the spot, so I reckon the future lies with white, rosé and fizz.

There have been a lot of plantings of so-called hybrid grape varieties such as Seyval Blanc which cope with our damp climate – although some say they don't have as much to offer as noble varieties.

But plantings of classics such as Chardonnay are on the up. In terms of flavour, you can generally expect English white wine to be similar to the flavour of the fruits that grow naturally in our hedgerows – crisp, bright and zingy with some aromatic twists.

As for the rosés, there are plenty out there to choose from and they tend to be tangy, fresh wines – think redcurrants and raspberries.

If you haven't tried an English fizz, there are a number of decent producers: look to Cornwall, Sussex and Kent and you won't go far wrong.

All of them have award-winning producers, making fizz with enough style and class to send your guests into a tizzy.

The chalky soil in southern England is similar to that of Champagne, and the temperature is on average only one degree centigrade cooler.

English wine still tends to be on the pricey side, but you can feel good about reducing your carbon footprint and supporting local produce – as well as tasting something seriously good.

Wrap up with a red wine in winter

With the leaves turning, a nip in the air and the first bonfire smoke drifting on the breeze, I'm always tempted to grab a coat, scarf and stout pair of boots to face the chill head-on.

But there's a far finer way to keep out the cold and indulge in a spot of luxuriant down time: a glass of red wine. Generally, wines with warming qualities are either from hotter climates and feature generous ripe flavours, or from grape varieties that are inherently spicy, such as Shiraz.

Shiraz – also known as Syrah when it is found in cooler climates – is one of my favourite red grape varieties. It usually has a gorgeous smoky streak running through it. It works brilliantly with roast red meats and steaks, and you can experiment with duck.

I've even found Syrah/Agiorgitiko blends from Greece that work magnificently when chilled: perfumed, sleek, full of flavour but with a real sense of finesse.

Syrah began its career in the northern Rhône – most famously in the appellation of Hermitage, but you may also have heard of St-Joseph and Cornas, which are also fantastic.

In Côte-Rôtie, winemakers often blend in a dash of the fragrant white grape Viognier, which adds a touch of aromatics.

Or you can hunt out bolder styles of Syrah from Chile, South Africa and Australia.

If you like the spice of Syrah, you could investigate South African

Pinotage, with its earthy edges, or Carmenère from Chile, with its peppery spice.

Or you could go for the plush richness of fruity Argentinean Malbec, a style that increasingly enthrals us.

It ranges from elegant and floral at higher altitudes to juicy and intense in hotter places such as Mendoza.

If you want to complement the glorious game that's on offer in winter, try Pinot Noir – a lighter style of wine, deft and zippy when young and much more savoury when aged.

German Pinot Noir is called Spätburgunder and (if you can find it on the shelves) is usually spicy and light. It's top with peppery duck.

My final tip is to think Portugal: there is, of course, port for deep winter, with its fruity spice, but more and more wineries are using port grapes to make standard reds rather than fortified wines.

Look for grape varieties such as Touriga Nacional and your autumn will start to sizzle.

When it comes to a good wine, what's in a name?

Wine is now such a status symbol that the act of spraying champagne all around has become the favoured way to show off wealth.

But how about wine as a different type of status symbol? For many celebrities, making wine and owning a vineyard is now an adjunct to a successful career.

Gérard Depardieu famously loves wine and has scores of winemaking projects, but you'd expect the wines of a Frenchman who loves flavour and cooking to be up to scratch.

Similarly, Rick Stein's Australian red and white are suitably Rick-ish in their down-to-earth manner.

More unexpected is wine from Vince Vineyards – that's Vince Neil of Mötley Crüe – proof that 'wine rocks'!

Meanwhile, Cliff Richard has his Portuguese Vida Nova wines, Sting is producing wine in Italy's Chianti region and Mick Hucknall introduced Il Cantante wine from Sicily. But the daddy of musical celebrity wine is Bob Dylan, whose name graces the Montepulciano of Fattoria Le Terrazze, branded as 'Planet Waves'.

In sport, the wine to seek out is from golfer Ernie Els. I recently visited his wine estate in South Africa and Ernie is not someone doing it out of vanity. With all the obligatory Ernie memorabilia, you might imagine it to be just a bit of a gimmick. It isn't. The winery is state of the art; the wine is good.

Sam Neill is the most famous actor producing wine; his

Two Paddocks Pinot Noir always performs well. And director Francis Ford Coppola prides himself on his estate in California.

Celebrity wine may not automatically have celebrity status but if it gets us all sampling good vino from round the world, it's on my VIP list.

Buyers and cellars: how best to store that quality bottle of wine

Gone are the days when every house had a cellar stuffed with dusty bottles waiting for the perfect moment to be cracked open. Wine is increasingly made for immediate consumption. That said, laying it down can be fun – but there are considerations before you buy.

First, where will you keep it?

Wine needs to be stored at around 11 degrees centigrade, but the key thing is to avoid sharp changes in temperature.

Never leave it in the attic (hot in summer, cold in winter) or in direct sunlight. You could invest in a wine fridge but generally wine just needs to be laid on its side somewhere cool and dark.

Alternatively, you could have someone store the wine for you. Plenty of companies provide professional cellarage services, charged per case per year, and as soon as you want the wine, it arrives on your doorstep.

Another option is to buy the wine before it's been bottled. This is known as buying *en primeur.*

You're betting on the quality in advance of tasting but if you stick to famous areas such as Bordeaux and big name producers, you shouldn't go far wrong.

The way it works is that you buy the wine at (hopefully) a cheaper price than it will cost on release. It is then delivered to the seller, who stores it for you. This is a top way to celebrate the birth of a child or a future anniversary.

Finally, choose your region carefully.

Invest in wines with serious structure and class, which will reveal hidden secrets as they age.

You can lay down red or sweet wines from Bordeaux and red or white from Burgundy.

Sweet wines from the Hungarian region of Tokaji develop beautifully over many years thanks to a thrilling balance of acidity and sugar.

Germany has a treasure trove of Riesling that works beautifully after a few years in the bottle.

And Italian Barolo is worth considering for laying down on account of its robust structure.

Match of the day: choosing the right food and drink combo

Matching food with wine can take your palate to another level. Combinations of texture, flavour and intensity can complement or contrast in a way that brings both the dish and the wine to life.

The simplest matches are often the best, for example, Spanish Fino sherry with a slice of jamón ibérico. Fino has a refreshing tang that partners the meat in an awesome duet of delight.

This match also adheres to one of my rules of thumb, which is to pair up food and drink from their place of origin.

More often than not, local recipes and wine styles have grown up and evolved together – for example, the famous Italian red Barolo partners exceptionally with porcini mushrooms and game thanks to its uniquely savoury flavour and aroma.

There are a number of myths surrounding wine and food matching, of which probably the biggest is that you should always go for red wine with cheese. Nonsense: goat's cheese is sublime with white Sauvignon Blanc, and sweet Hungarian Tokaji or French Sauternes make thrillingly contrasting matches with salty Stilton.

But there are flavours that are deemed to be virtually impossible to match up, such as artichoke and asparagus.

However, there is a secret weapon in your arsenal: Grüner Veltliner. It's an Austrian white grape producing dry wines with a white peppery touch.

In addition to flavour, consider the texture of a dish: is it crunchy, squidgy, dense or light?

All these elements give clues as to whether you should match a light simple wine or a richer, heavier candidate.

The very best way to learn is to experiment as much as possible – and I'll drink to that!

Come on baby light my fire...
wine with that added spice

I'm a huge fan of spice in my food, whether it comes from horseradish, jalapeños or peppercorns – but spice in wine is just as thrilling.

Spicy flavours often come from the grape variety itself, as in the case of Grenache with its white pepper edge, or Syrah/Shiraz (same grape, different name) which often has a smoky, charry tang.

You can also find leathery and earthy spices in wines that have been aged for a while (as in the case of Spanish Gran Reserva Riojas) or more truffly scents (as in Italian Barolo) and even cigar-box-type smells (red wines from Bordeaux). White wine spice tends to be less evident, though oak can give a gingery edge to richer wines and some grapes have a fragrant exotic spice (in particular, I'm thinking of Gewürztraminer).

Some countries pump out more spicy wine than others and generally it's those with intense sunlight on their side. Chile is famous for Carmenère with its peppery kick. That said, when unripe it can be revoltingly bitter so pick your winemaker with care.Syrah from Chile is also worth hunting down, from regions such as Limari and Elqui. The best of these examples have a lovely smoky richness.

South African reds get a lot of stick for their trademark 'earthy' edge, but there are some brilliantly spicy Cape reds to get stuck into, especially if you're a fan of generous fruit and a warming edge.

You could also consider sampling Aussie reds, which are generally as hearty and friendly as their larger-than-life countrymen. New Zealand also has a fair few spicy wines, such as Syrah from the Hawke's Bay region.

Whichever country you go for, as soon as you catch a whiff of bonfire on the breeze or spicy cooking wafting from an open door, dose up on a spicy wine and get stuck into a bonfire banger!

Top of the pops: champagne alternatives

Champagne isn't getting any cheaper, and increasingly we're looking for good value alternatives. But do they really hit the spot?

The traditional way of making champagne is to ferment a still white wine, then add yeast and sugar into each bottle for a secondary fermentation.

A popular alternative to champagne is Spanish cava, which is made in the same way but from Spanish grape varieties; they are crisp with a hint of aromatics.

If you prefer a more complex drop, there are Gran Reservas, which are cavas aged for a minimum of 30 months, or you could hunt a fruity pink cava to make a festive change.

There's no denying Italian Prosecco is fun and frothy and inexpensive. It's not champagne, of course — for starters it's made from the Glera grape and is made using a different method, which allows for the secondary fermentation in big tanks. But if you're after a light crisp sipper and a real bang for your buck, Prosecco is hard to beat.

And for food matching, try it with a slice of fresh buffalo mozzarella — it's a revelation and makes a great start to the night if you're entertaining at home.

Then there's French crémant. This is a French sparkling wine produced outside of the Champagne region yet made in the same way.

You can find different styles from Burgundy, Alsace and the Loire but my tip is to hunt for fizz from Limoux, a place stacked with know-how as it lays claim to being the first area to have produced sparkling wine.

Or you could look to the New World for fizz made in the same way – from New Zealand or California, for example.

They are all unique styles and whatever your budget, there's a fizz out there to froth up your fiesta.

Try some aroma therapy with these sublime white wines

Aromatic whites. You might not be buying them because their names are hard to say, come from obscure places or the labels don't give much of an idea of what to expect. However, if you know what to seek, wines in this style are a bit like *The Secret Millionaire*, tucked away on the shelves waiting for you to get close... with no hint of the hidden riches on offer.

Aromatic white grapes come in all shapes and sizes, from full-on floral belters such as Gewürztraminer to those with a more subtle aromatic quality such as Viognier. The latter is a passion of mine; when it's done right, it's sublime, with hints of apricot and honeysuckle.

I've been enjoying Viognier from Chile for a while but there are some belters from France's Languedoc, too. It's a great one to try with mild Asian cooking as it has roundness along with its mild aromatic streak. Condrieu in France produces posh Viognier and it's one I sometimes pick from restaurant wine lists as it can be a bargain in comparison with super famous wines.

Another couple of grapes to sample with mildly aromatic flavours are Marsanne and Roussanne, which can be richly textured and peachy.

For a grape variety with a unique orange blossom floral aroma but that tends to be dry on the palate, experiment with Argentinian Torrontés. It's amazingly fragrant and can be a wonderful aperitif, especially the crisper ones.

Prices are generally great value and it pairs well with a wide range of dishes from ceviche to fragrant Thai food. Another cracking grape to check out is the chameleon-like Chenin Blanc, which in the Loire makes dry, sparkling and sweet wine.

I reckon it's reached a special place in South Africa with styles ranging from rich and fruity right through to the lean and pure with a mineral ping.

Back in Europe, my old favourite from Austria, Grüner Veltliner, has a white pepper touch, while German Rieslings can possess a sublime aromatic quality and offer some serious value for money. But Riesling in itself is a whole other column.

For now, I urge you to raise your glass and sample an aromatic white, out of the norm and into the future.

Licence to thrill: where best to buy your bottle of wine

There are some splendid off-licences and independent wine shops offering good value and characterful wines to sample. But are they on the slide? Over the years, lots of familiar high street chains have gone into administration – which is a shame, because we wine fans need as many outlets as possible to choose booze from.

The vast majority of wine bought in this country comes from supermarkets. The big message about your local off-licence is to make sure you use it – the staff are there to engage with you and help you make the right choice.

There are many ways to remove the sense of risk out of buying a bottle you might not normally consider, but talking to the guys behind the counter is a top way to start. That's how it happened to me, in an Oddbins in Edinburgh in 1994. The assistant was laid-back, welcoming, T-shirted and stubbly, and with jazz playing it all created an environment that didn't feel in the least bit elitist or intimidating. There were wines on taste every Saturday then. That day, I tasted a bottle of white wine for around three quid and it changed my life. I thought it was thrilling, great value and something I could share with my mates.

Oddbins was a high street and trade favourite for years, then it took a regrettable nosedive, losing a huge streak of the quirk and fun and, crucially, quality that had blazed such an imaginative and inspiring trail.

However, it then changed ownership and has been improving significantly.

As far as chains go, in recent times, Majestic has been fantastic at giving its staff training, and the knowledge and enthusiasm in-store is impressive – and you can now buy a case of six different bottles of wine instead of 12, so get in there. The range is diverse and it's consistently good at offering intelligent offers.We need diversity, so buy wine from off-licences, independent wine merchants and supermarkets, too – they are all aiming to supply the wines their customers want to drink.

Check out your local indies and offies, even if it's just the local corner shop or convenience store.

Use it or lose it!

Blend it, shake it: it's all in the grapes

Every year, I blend the Porta Palo wines for the P&O Cruises fleet, and it's awesome fun, a bit like building a recipe. In some ways, wine is easier to understand if it's a single grape variety such as Shiraz or Chardonnay, as you can identify the leading characteristic.

But wine is also made from blends of grapes, which offers a tailored, unique approach. Take Rioja: it's a region that pumps out many styles of juice, the majority of which are blended from grapes such as Tempranillo, Garnacha, Mazuelo and Graciano. Why? Different varieties bring different qualities to a blend – colour, zip, spice, fruit and structure. Their sum is greater than the parts.

The Champagne region is a fantastic example of blending not just different grape varieties (Chardonnay, Pinot Noir, Pinot Meunier) but also blending across grapes from different years for the non-vintage wines (NV on the label). The reason for this is genius – it maintains a consistent house style and flavour, so when you buy NV champagne, you know you'll be getting the same taste, year in year out.

This was a blending model that the Aussies used for a lot of their everyday wine for years. Each year they'd make sure the style was consistent by sourcing fruit from a wide area of vineyards, so that people who bought it could feel confident that it would taste like it did the previous year.

I've always been a fan of sampling music before I buy an album and I am delighted that more and more wine shops are offering the chance to try before you buy. Thanks to modern dispensing systems, wines can be pumped out by the glass in pristine order, so you don't have to buy the whole bottle to know what you're getting – and with blended wines, that opens the doors to a world of experimentation, rummaging and glugging. Finding your sweet spot just got a whole lot simpler.

If you're still unsure, try established blends from regions steeped in tradition such as Chianti (where blends are founded on the Sangiovese grape along with other local varieties) and Bordeaux, where Cabernet Sauvignon and Merlot are the principal grapes used in reds (but you can also find Cabernet Franc, Petit Verdot, Carmenère and Malbec). What you're looking for in the wine is a sense of balance.

And if you really want to branch out, look to some of the quirkier blends coming out of Australia and New Zealand, where the sense of flare and experimentation is modern and thrilling – and produces some fascinating results.

How to fill 12 splendid hours of festive drinking

No, we're not suggesting you wolf down this lot on Christmas Day – this festive drinks guide simply weighs up the wonderful options on the big day, from the fizz with the smoked salmon through to scotch at the midnight hour.

Christmas! It's not only the time of year to get reacquainted with the best of the Bond films (you can't beat *Goldfinger* and *The Spy Who Loved Me*) but also the time to splash out on some extra fine wine to share with those who deserve it: loved ones, close mates, accountants and easy-going bosses all spring to mind.

You don't have to spend a fortune on wine to maximise your festive fun. The best plan is to work out how many people you're expecting to pour for, and how fancy you want to go. For example, if you're having a bunch of mates round and it's an easy night of revels, some fizz and a few bottles of decent red will do the trick.

Of course, for the big day itself, you'll want to make sure you've got the best. And that's where I come in. You want booze that's good value – and tastes fantastic.

I've got suggestions to take you from noon till night. I'm not recommending, of course, that you drink every bottle on the page – although a drop of each would make it a truly memorable day...

The Smoked Salmon

Well, some say it's got to be champagne and that nothing else goes with smoked salmon quite as magnificently. To stand out from the crowd, why not go for an English fizz (also good for toasting the Queen's speech)? Some are so good I reckon they rival decent vintage champagne. For a change, you could choose a zinging dry Aussie Riesling from the Clare Valley.

Christmas Lunch

As Christopher Lee so memorably put it in *The Man With The Golden Gun*, 'this is the part I really like'. It is the one day of the year when I am allowed – no, encouraged to – go wild on wine and splash out on some real stunners. For me, that doesn't mean buying big bling brands, but selecting something extraordinary to indulge in.

I remember one year sampling three different Pinot Noirs with the turkey, one from France, one from New Zealand and one from Germany. The whole family got stuck into a fantastic rant about which one was best. Turns out all three had their champions in the Smith family and we had to open several subsequent bottles just to make sure. With turkey, it's a great opportunity to open a few bottles and allow people to mix and match.

Generally if you're having meaty stuffing (eg, sausage or liver), go for a gamey red wine such as an awesomely classy red Burgundy from Vosne-Romanée Premier Cru, or try a New Zealand stunner from Central Otago.

If you're having a fruity stuffing (such as apricots) then go for a rich white with a dose of oak. White grape varieties from the Rhône such as Marsanne and Roussanne are great – and there are some stunning examples from Australia and South Africa.

Or you could opt for a classy Burgundian Chardonnay, or a world class alternative from New Zealand, which put a lot of top white Burgundies to shame – zinging, pure, elegant, complex and about as good as Chardonnay gets.

Finally, if you're going for a spicy stuffing with your turkey then sparkling Shiraz can be fun – it's a bit like Marmite: people tend to love it or hate it. I often serve it between cheese and pudding, as a pre-dessert palate – think of it as a bramble sorbet and you'll get on with it much better.

Christmas Pudding

Wow, what a massive texture Christmas pudding can be! Pull out the big guns such as Australian Liqueur Muscat – think sweet coffee and fig richness. Alternatively, Pedro Ximénez sherry is stuffed full of figgy and sweet date flavours, and it works fabulously with Christmas pud.

The Cheese Course

There are a few options here. Tawny port is wonderful with Stilton, or if you want to amp it up, Late Bottled Vintage port offers terrific value.

Tokaji works too, and it's one of my favourite sweet wines from Hungary. An absolute Christmas treat would be a glass or two of really old 6 Puttonyos Tokaji – top notch Tokaji has the potential to outlive us all. It's sweetly balanced with zing, and layered with savoury nutty character as well as being utterly mouth-watering.

Digestifs

After all that feasting, you need to be congratulated with a soothing glass or two of mellow indulgence. Cream liqueurs are popular but for me, whisky is the ultimate settler and drink to reflect with. My favourites tend to be peaty with spicy touches and a fruity edge. Beautiful.

Nightcap

For a late night treat, switch to a 12-year-old single malt from Islay which can be so highly complex they're like a novel in a glass, and would make a fantastic Christmas gift for... well, me. Cheers!

The chill-out zone

The festive season doesn't start and end with Christmas Day, as it stretches all the way from mid-December into the New Year. After a guide to Christmas Day's best drinks, it's time to settle at a cruising speed on our journey towards 2010.

For a mid-holiday gathering of friends you need some fizz, and Prosecco does the trick. It's great value, with lively pear and sherbet freshness. Next up, whites and reds. For whites, you want something light, simple and crisp. Italian whites can work a treat. Pinot Grigio is a crowd-pleaser but tends to taste of virtually nothing, so check out white grapes such as Verdicchio, Grillo, Falanghina or Fiano – they shouldn't cost you any more.

Keep reds fruity and drinkable; don't worry about spending a wad of cash on aged beauties – this is a party, so the wine's going to get glugged and spilled. South America is a winner for simple, enjoyable reds, as is the Languedoc region of France.

But how about Spain? A Tempranillo (the headline grape of Rioja) can be mellow and superb to sip at a shindig.

Port

Tawny port makes a decent aperitif chilled and served in small doses with salted almonds. For a sensational treat, grab a tangy and svelte 20-year-old Tawny port. Or try Late Bottled Vintage for a fuller-bodied style.

Sherry

For aperitifs, stick with Fino or Manzanilla – chilled right down and served with green olives.

Broaden your wine horizons

One of the best bits about wine is exploring the new frontiers of discovery.

Instead of settling for the same old bottle clinking into your trolley week in, week out, let us stand together here and now, united in our pledge to broaden our wine horizons and try something different.

Chenin Blanc, for example, is a terrific grape to discover if you're a fan of Chardonnay. Chenin has a laudable chameleon-like ability to turn itself into wines of all different shapes and sizes, from bone dry belters to more oaky luxuriant full whites.

If you want to taste pristine modern Chenin, South Africa is pumping out some absolute gems.

If you're a fan of bone dry wines, Albariño from Galicia in Spain is definitely worth hunting down. Albariño (pronounced al-bar-ee-nyo) is increasingly widely available both in stores and on wine lists.

The UK's passion for Pinot Grigio knows no bounds – but Italy is stacked with alternative whites. Fiano from Sicily is a total winner, offering good value and joyful bright fruit flavours, while Falanghina delivers a peachy whirl of mouth-watering flavours.

Sauvignon Blanc from New Zealand is also mightily popular. But have you thought about sampling Sauvignon Gris? It's got a bit more weight and there are some terrific examples from France and Chile.

As for reds, if you're a fan of Shiraz, Chile also offers the Carmenère grape, which has a similar peppery kick. But if it's smoke and earthiness you're after, take another look at South African Pinotage, a cross between Pinot Noir and Cinsault.

If mellow Merlot is more your cup of tea, then Malbec from high in the Argentinian Andes may put a spring in your step. And for fans of Italian Barolo, there's Greek Xinomavro, which has a similar tendency towards savoury edges with a medium body but powerful structure.

A dose of red heat

Firm frost, flurrying snow and ever the risk of icy drizzle. Insulation is called for and I say we pour ourselves a glass or two of big warming red.

There are a few things that make a wine warming – not least where it's produced. In warmer climates, the heat generates more sugar in the grapes, and so more alcohol. There's usually also bold flavour and body to match.

We all know which regions are cooler (northern France, for example) and which are hotter (southern Spain). We also know it's fresher by the seaside and up mountains it gets chillier. With all this in mind, you can investigate local wines with a better idea of what to expect – less alcohol and more zip in cooler regions, more alcohol and bolder flavours from hotter ones.

Australia is one place we Brits love to buy from – we admire the consistency and affordability of their fun wines. Oz has recently hit some hard times, but for warming reds there's still plenty on offer from regions such as the Barossa valley near Adelaide, which pumps out Shiraz so mighty it's practically got hooves.

Nearer home, Spain has lots of warming reds, especially from areas such as Priorat. And let's not forget France: think of Châteauneuf-du-Pape, its vineyards covered in magical 'pudding stones' that hold the day's warmth, at night radiating the heat, giving ripe, intense wines capable of long ageing. South Africa, California and Argentina also have hotter regions ideal for bold flavours and charging up vines with a warming sense of oomph.

Grape varieties can also help you find more warming flavours. Shiraz is deep and peppery, Cabernet Sauvignon, with its blackcurranty intensity, can be depth-charged with seriously chunky body, and Argentinean Malbec is also worth probing for a dose of winter warmth with black fruit appeal. Grenache can also get quite high in alcohol, especially form Australia.

All these grapes, while magnified in warmer climates, are also found in cooler places for wines that are less full-on, so depending on your taste, you'll be able to find one to suit your mood.

The association of regions with a particular style counts for a great deal too. Barolo in Italy has long been known for wines that are pale yet highly structured and stacked with tannin and power, thanks to the Nebbiolo grape. More recently, South Africa's Swartland has gained a reputation for quality Syrah.

Most warming of all is port: sweet, rich and fortified and one of Portugal's great exports. Late Bottled Vintage port can offer serious value, while sipping chilled Tawny port with a bowl of salted almonds by the banks of the Douro river is one of life's unmissable treats.

However, if port's too high octane for you, Portugal has red wines from the same grapes but left unfortified. You may find them blended together along with a squirt of something like Cabernet Sauvignon.

Sugar & spice: how to match dessert wines with the right foods

Loving dessert wine can make you feel like you're all alone, twiddling your thumbs and counting coconuts on a desert island.

They are not, let's face it, the height of fashion; these days most of us prefer a cool glass of dry white to a rich glass of sticky goo.

Which is a pity, because not all dessert wines are treacly, honey-like elixirs that will glue your tongue to the roof of your mouth.

One overlooked classic dessert wine is champagne. Some examples can work beautifully with pudding or alongside rich flavours. Look for 'demi-sec' on a champagne label and try serving a glass or two at the end of a meal for a refreshing, fruity and bubbly treat.

The key to dessert wines is context. Alongside food they can be sublime: either to work with the sweetness of a dish, or to contrast; a sweet Sauternes with a salty Roquefort is one of the greatest gastronomic collisions on the planet.

The key here with the cheese and the Sauternes is the similar intensity of flavour and complementary textures. Both are rich and creamy, and the sweet and salt balance is impeccable. For top value, check out Australia's answer to Sauternes, Botrytis Semillon, which is often outstanding value.

We create these kinds of contrasts in cooking all the time without batting an eyelid. Think of chutney, with contrasting sugary fruit and tangy vinegar within it, then served with a creamy, spicy curry, building layer upon layer of contrasts. We love it.

For lovers of foie gras, ethically sourced or traditional, my favourite wine match is Tokaji Aszu from Hungary. The texture of the wine is as sleek and unctuous as the dish and the naturally high acidity of the grapes helps to cut through each mouthful.

The sweetness of Tokaji Aszu is measured in *puttonyos*, with six as the maximum sweetness. I find in general the balance of a top quality Tokaji works best at around five *puttonyos* but I urge to you taste them through for yourself to find your sweet spot. Essencia from the Tokaji region is even sweeter and highly prized; it's a dessert in its own right.

The other super-cool thing about Tokaji is that it lasts for decades in the cellar thanks to the preserving effect of the sugar and acidity. It develops from fruity-sweet, jammy glory into amazing layers of nut and tobacco-like savouriness. You can also delve into the pure glory of Icewine from Canada, Trockenbeerenauslese from Germany and Vin Santo from Italy. Everyone's at it.

Fortified wines are another potential area. Port is often maligned as the tipping drink of the night that kicks off brutal hangovers. So why not make it the first drink of the night and sip a chilled glass of Tawny port alongside a bowl of salted almonds?

Sherry, too, is not just for grannies. You can get bone dry sherries (Fino and Manzanilla) but there are some awesome sweet Olorosos. Then there is Pedro Ximénez, which is like a sticky black syrup of dates and figs. Pour it over vanilla ice cream – delicious!

The world of sweet wines is out there, and they're an awesome accompaniment to shake off the winter blues.

Out of Africa

I once spent a week in South Africa pretending to be on holiday but I ended up doing quite a bit of wine tasting and visiting wineries.

My Dad came with me and we had a blast – there is an enthusiastic buzz around South African winemaking. There is confidence – not just in know-how and delivering quality wine, but in a pioneering sense of adventure.

Part of South Africa's conundrum is the huge range of soils they have – a jigsaw for winemakers that takes years to piece together. That said, already you can see trends emerging, even in regions that have only recently been planted with vines.

Cooler climate areas such as Hemel-en-Aarde and Elgin are gaining a reputation for zinging Sauvignon Blanc and reds with a sense of freshness; warmer places, such as the vineyards in Swartland are pumping some plumper Syrah along with whites such as Chenin Blanc blended with such grapes as Viognier, Clairette, Grenache Blanc, Marsanne, Roussanne and more.

The potential for blending ground-breaking and uniquely South African wines is huge. Semillon seems to do brilliantly in South Africa and I'd love to see a whole lot more of it –there are some crackers from the Constantia region.

Chenin Blanc and Syrah are the two grapes for white and red that I loved the most on my trip. Both achieve stylistic differences depending on where they're grown, and they withstand the climate admirably.

But for me, blends remain key turf to push the boundaries of South African wine.

It's for keeps: how to save wine for another day

As soon as you open a bottle of wine, it starts to change; as oxygen interacts with the wine, it begins to develop and alter in flavour.

The shift is subtle for the first few minutes, and a bit of oxygen can actually help chunky red wines to soften up. But after a few days left open, you can bet that it will taste less like vino and more like vinegar.

Sometimes it's nice to have a single glass rather than guzzling the whole bottle, or to match different wines with different dishes. On these occasions you could simply replace the cork, but that doesn't do much to stop the wine interacting with the air you've already let into the bottle. Fear not – help is at hand.

If money is no object, you could look into installing an automated preservation system. OK, so they cost several thousand pounds, but the idea is that you have a cabinet that stores your open bottles of wine at the correct temperature and dispenses them by the glass. The wine is preserved in the bottle with inert gas and lasts more than three weeks. Pretty cool kit.

You can increasingly see them in action in bars and shops around the country. Here you'll have the chance to sample wines that might otherwise be too expensive by the bottle. I'd love to see more of these systems in restaurants across the country so we can mix and match wines with our meals.

But let's face it, not all of us are going to invest such a substantial sum of money to preserve our weeknight bottle of vino. The best alternative to simply shoving the cork back in and crossing your fingers is to use a bottle stopper that really fits the bottle. But this won't, in truth, buy you a huge amount of time. Vacuum pump systems are inexpensive and work pretty well. The idea is that you suck the air out of a bottle and seal it with a rubber stopper.

White wines can be kept fresh in the fridge, but a longer lasting option are small cabinet systems that create a vacuum in a bottle, which should keep wine for up to ten days.

For champagne and sparkling wines, there are various fizz-stoppers that help retain the sparkle – you can find them on the shelves of supermarkets and wine retailers. They work fairly well, though in my experience, a bottle of fizz once opened tends to vanish in mere moments...

The most successful method of preserving a wine at home is to use a canister of inert gas that has a long thin tube attached to the nozzle – rather like a can of WD40 – that you direct into the wine bottle. A couple of squirts later and your wine is covered with a layer of the inert gas that stops oxygen getting near it.

'Winesave' is what I use at home to seal my bottles (you can find it online), and the wine is good for least three days, maybe more. I'll sometimes have as many as ten bottles on the go all at once so that I can match a glass or two with whatever dish I'm serving – and no wasted wine.

Point Blanc: the grapes of pleasure when it comes to wine

Aaah: Sauvignon Blanc. If one grape variety encapsulates exuberant refreshment, zing and crisp citrus glory, this is it. If you've ever dozily chomped on a grapefruit at the breakfast table, you'll know what I mean.

Turbo-charged wake-up juice, a mouth-watering aperitif for the hearty feast, it's best known from France's Loire valley: Sancerre, elegant, crisp and elfish, or Pouilly-Fumé with its smoky twist.

You can also find good value by looking for Sauvignon de Touraine. Every northern French Sauvignon Blanc has a bright citrus ping, which is a fantastic match with goat's cheese.

But the grape has been highly successful beyond France. Marlborough, a tiny region on the tip of New Zealand's South Island, has an international reputation for high quality, uniquely flavoursome Sauvignon Blanc.

South Africa's Sauvignon Blanc range of styles is somewhere between Loire elegance and New Zealand fruitiness – check out the Elgin or Hemel-En-Aarde regions.

In Chile, a winemaking paradise thanks to its soil and climate range, Sauvignon Blanc thrives with pure freshness and a green pepper spiciness.

The Leyda coast grows a sublime Sauvignon grape. The Pacific Ocean acts like a giant air conditioning unit on the vineyards.

The effect is electrifying: racy, thrilling wines.

Up in Chile's north, the Limari valley is a near-desert region creating intense Sauvignon Blanc with a near-salty tinge to the powerful citrus thrust. It's sensational with a plate of lime infused fresh fish ceviche.

Usually Sauvignon Blanc is served young and fresh, such as those also from Western Australia or northern Italy. I've even tasted a German Sauvignon Blanc from Bavaria.

However, some have been romping in oak barrels to get a fleshy nutty edge. From the US, look out for Fumé Blanc to experience this style.

However it is handled, the bright exuberance of Sauvignon Blanc is the perfect refresher for days that need a dose of sunshine.

Why real romantics say it with vins d'amour on Valentine's Day

So what exactly is a romantic wine? For me, it's a wine that, no matter what colour or strength, will discreetly wreathe the moment in quality and magic. Now, you could just buy a fine wine and hope for the best.

But if you can show that you've thought about your lover's tastes, carefully selected a tipple to appeal especially to them or considered matching the wine to a romantic dinner that you've made, you can quadruple your brownie points in a heartbeat.

Of course, there are some lovely pink champagnes around, or if you're feeling patriotic, there's some English pink fizz worth sampling, with bright, strawberry-ish, crisp refreshment. And if you're after a bargain, you could consider rosé cava or Prosecco.

Beyond fizz, there's a world of wines to choose from, and you should match your choice to the setting, mood and character of your planned event. Think along the lines of what your partner would really love – then surprise them.

For example, if they're a fan of light, crisp Italian Pinot Grigio, try a glass of Falanghina with its subtle aromatic twist. If spicy Shiraz is a winner, consider Carmenère from Chile, or Malbec or Tannat from Argentina. And if Chardonnay floats their boat, South African Chenin Blanc is always ready to leap off the shelves.

When quality is the name of the game there's always a safety net in choosing from the French classics: Chablis, Pinot Noir from

Burgundy or red Bordeaux blends. But these wines can be pricey, and if you're after a romantic tipple that won't break the bank, you could look elsewhere in France.

For example, if you're a fan of Châteauneuf-du-Pape but less enamoured with its hefty price tag, grab a humbler Rhône red from the villages of Cairanne or Rasteau.

Also, consider Spain for romantic tipples. Rioja offers a wealth of styles to choose from: crisp whites, rosés, young reds, aged reds and everything in between.

Meanwhile, there are lots of other fabulous options to explore, from traditional sherry (chilled Fino or Manzanilla makes an awesome romantic aperitif) to more vibrant whites, such as Albariño from Galicia, to stunning red blends from Priorat.

Alternatively, you could investigate bespoke tipples from off the beaten track. Irsai Oliver is a floral, aromatic dry white wine from Hungary that's perfect with mildly spicy dishes.

Good wine at a gorgeous price – let's drink to love!

Great whites: the perfect wine to welcome the sun

When spring is about to make her big entrance, I love sipping rich white wines bold enough to keep out the cold and bright enough to give a glimpse of the sunshine about to peep through the clouds.

Bigness in white wine can cover lots of different aspects – the texture, the alcohol content and the intensity of the flavour. This can be governed by a number of things, but one aspect that certainly helps the grapes is regular doses of sunshine. White grapes that come from cooler places tend to be bright and zingy, but if there's a dose of heat even white grapes can develop some seriously bold flavour.

And if the wine producer is prepared to leave the grapes on the vines for a bit longer, their sugar levels increase and create wines of serious richness.

One region that excels at producing rich whites is Alsace. The grape varieties commonly found in white wines from here tend to be quite striking in flavour – Muscat with its orangey twinge, Riesling with its zing and curious diesel and boot-polish aroma when aged, Gewürztraminer with its rose floral glory (a great match with powerful cheese) and Pinot Gris - with fabulous pear and floral flavours, rich texture and a sublime match for mildly spiced dishes.

It's not always easy to tell how sweet or dry a wine from Alsace is going to be. But if you ask your local merchant and are prepared to expect a degree of ripeness in most wines, you're in for a journey of discovery. Alsace Grand Cru is the top stuff and if you see Vendange Tardive on the label, it's a late harvest wine that's likely to be a touch sweet. Sélection de Grains Nobles is properly sweet and can be seriously high in alcohol.

Away from Alsace, Gewürztraminer is capable of rich texture and full-on aromatic and floral flavour. You can find good value examples from Chile, from regions such as Bío-Bío. Chile is also coming up with some interesting examples of Riesling and I've had some good examples of Gewürztraminer from New Zealand.

Another grape with a fleshy character and peachy flavours is Marsanne. It can work well on its own to produce fleshy round whites that are great with white meats. Also consider Roussanne, which is one of the blending grapes in white Châteauneuf-du-Pape – a blend that's well worth considering for springtime, with its roundness and sunshine-fuelled rich fruit flavours.

Chardonnay, too, can be rich, especially when it grows in warm climates from places such as Argentina and California. It can develop rich toasty character and some serious texture.

Chardonnay can also make powerful champagne – especially when blended with Pinot Noir and Pinot Meunier – red grapes that can add richness and power. Champagne is a wonderfully rich fizz thanks to a high proportion of Pinot Noir. It's a fantastic way to kiss goodbye to winter.

From Piedmont to Sicily – every corner of Italy offers a wine you can't refuse

The thing that makes me whoop with delight about Italian wine is the sheer range of styles on offer and the wealth of grape varieties.

Rich reds, crisp whites, sweet wines, fizz, you name it, Italy can do it – and with fierce pride in the quality of regional diversity.

As I type this I'm on a plane heading south to Sicily. While speeding above the mountainous north, I'm swooping over the hills of Piedmont with its world famous Barolo wine.

Nebbiolo is the grape behind this wine that's pale in colour but mighty in structure. 2004 was a cracking year for Barolo.

Truffles are a powerful and pungent flavour, which generally a red wine stands up to best – Barolo is the perfect candidate, or you could try Barbaresco, which is also made from the Nebbiolo grape and sometimes a touch softer than Barolo.

Northern Italy is by no means only about red wine. You can find stunning whites – everything from Pinot Grigio to Friulano and even zippy and crisp Riesling.

Pinot Grigio can be underwhelmingly neutral but the finest examples come from the north – check out Pinot Grigio from Alto Adige, which can be a world away from the water-like offerings that are all too often sloshed into our glasses.

Veneto is the place to hunt Prosecco – bargain bubbly that is brilliant to customise with fruit purée to create cocktails such as the famous

Bellini based on peach purée.

I'm landing in Bologna to change flights. My connection gives enough time to pop into town for lunch – what else but the local spaghetti Bolognese – and a chance to reflect on the wines lurking further south in Tuscany and beyond.

Chianti is a style of red that has a trademark sour cherry tang to it that works well matched with tomato based sauces. Brunello di Montalcino is based on the same Sangiovese grape as Chianti and commands high prices for its ageworthiness.

The region of Maremma has become famous for super-Tuscan wines such as Sassicaia and Ornellaia, turbocharged with rich fruit and hunted as cult wines by collectors and fans.

Back on the plane, high above Marche, I look out for whites such as Verdicchio dei Castelli di Jesi as a crisp dry alternative to Pinot Grigio.

Puglia has some great value vino on offer and is a place to watch. Consider the region of Campania for mildly aromatic whites such as Falanghina.

I finally touch down in Sicily at dusk. Sicily is a world of wine in itself, from the local dry whites such as Grecanico, Fiano and Grillo to svelte red Nero D'Avola and floral red Cerasuolo di Vittoria.

I'm dining on the south coast tonight on the beach next to Porta Palo in da Vittorio Ristorante. It's by no means a flash joint but a regular haunt of mine and the home of some of the world's greatest and freshest fish – and well worth a visit for an evening feast with a few glasses of Sicilian glory and the rousing cry of, 'Salute!' echoing across the fishing port into the night.

The big bangs: for wine that packs a huge punch, try a bottle from a volcanic region

Volcanoes are awesome. They're cauldrons of energetic destruction, but they also unleash energy and life and create soil that produces unique wines with stacks of character.

I've been fascinated by volcanoes ever since I was 19, when I climbed Mount Merapi in Java during a minor eruption. You needn't be dodging lava to appreciate their power, though – you can feel the Earth flexing its mighty muscles by sampling a glass of intense volcanic vino.

The long term impact of volcanoes on soil and wine production is extraordinary. Vineyards situated on volcanic soils usually produce intensely flavoured wines with striking personality.

The number of volcanic wine producing regions is amazing. Millions of years ago, California's Napa valley was an area of huge volcanic activity, many of the vineyards of Chile have volcanic soil, and there's a winery in Hawaii that calls itself 'Volcano Winery'.

You can also look a lot closer to home to find volcanic wines of astonishing impact.

We've got some beautiful volcanic vineyards in Europe, in countries such as Germany, Hungary and Italy. Perhaps my favourite volcano wine comes from the Greek holiday island of Santorini. After the eruption that took place around 1500 BC, the island was covered in ash and pumice, which laid the foundations for some of the world's most unique vineyards.

The local white grape variety Assyrtiko copes amazingly growing in the volcanic soil, with living vines woven into basket shapes to keep them cool, producing zinging white wines of serious intensity and class.

With no irrigation and low rainfall, the vineyards often rely on moisture from sea mist, which is said to give some wines a bone dry salty tang.

If you are lucky enough to find yourself on the island, try the sweet wines too, which are lusciously sweet and have a terrific zippy tang due to fermenting the grapes after a period drying in the hot sun.

Italy too has some magical wines produced from vines in volcanic regions. Greco di Tufo comes from vineyards that thrive in the volcanic soil around Avellino in Campania.

This crisp dry beauty is charged with energy and mineral power and is great with seafood.

Sicily is another huge wine producing area, and home to Mount Etna, whose slopes are peppered with vineyards.

According to Homer, it was wine from Etna that Odysseus poured to get the Cyclops hammered so he could escape being eaten alive. I've tasted white wines from Etna grapes, such as Minella, with pristine purity and potency, and reds with a uniquely spicy intensity, and I can see how the Cyclops found it hard to resist their charms.

If you're a fan of full-on flavour and up for tasting some of the world's most unforgettable wines, then shake up your palate with some volcano power – it goes all the way up to 11.

Seven Heaven: treat yourself to a fine wine for just £7

The truth is, when you buy a bottle of wine, you're secretly not paying for wine at all. I know it sounds odd, but when you break it down, a huge proportion of your outlay on your Friday night tipple is covering VAT, duty, import costs, marketing and a host of other hidden price boosters.

Duty, VAT and mark-ups from high street chains all take their toll. Take into account the exchange rate, and if you spend £5 on a bottle of wine you can bet you're only really paying about 80p to the winery. That covers pruning, manpower, barrels, machinery, pest control in the vineyard, glass for the bottles, lab kit, label design and finally, wine.

But if you spend £7, a huge chunk of that extra cash goes on the wine itself. The fact is, when you spend a pound or two more, investment in the quality of your wine skyrockets. The sweet spot for buying wine in the UK is £10, and there are still some belters to be had for £7.

I'm generally not a big fan of discount offers on the high street. There's usually a reason why the wine is down in price – either it's a marketing ploy to persuade you to buy more than you planned to, or the wine is about to be replaced with a more recent vintage.

Another way to maximise your spend at £7 is to buy more than one bottle at a time. Most supermarkets will offer you a case discount.

However you buy your wine, the important thing is that you spend a bit of money on the wine in the bottle, and not just on the piggyback costs.

Spring uncorked: a host of optimistic wines to welcome a new season

When the snowdrops in your garden have been and gone, the crocuses are up and the daffodils are about to burst into flower, the time has come to crack open those rare and curious wines that smell of flowers, freshness and all things uplifting.

Torrontés is one of my current favourites. It's a white grape variety from Argentina with an aromatic edge – think lemon Turkish delight – but when you sip it, it can be lean, bright and illuminating. It's a gem of a wine, but not one to bother ageing in your cellar. Just pop it in the fridge, knock up a stir-fry packed with lemon grass and sip the taste of spring.

If you're after a red, you can sometimes find floral notes in Argentinian Malbec, or you could consider hunting in France's northern Rhône around places such as Crozes-Hermitage, where they make Syrah that can sometimes smell as flowery as lilac.

They can be pricey, but the best examples are laced with ingenious complexity that makes you want to toss your Dickens novel into the fire and concentrate solely on the vino in your glass. Cherry-like with almondy niffs, when you sip it it's boom time – lilac, peppery flashes and a sense of vivid, living fruit flavour.

If your blood pressure requires you spend a touch less on your springtime fix of floral vino, then check out Dolcetto. It's an awesome lighter style of red from Italy, found in Piedmont – damson-y and floral, offering a bright tang and joyful fruit without being heavy. You could try serving it chilled in hotter weather, just like Beaujolais.

It can be tricky to pick out a winning Beaujolais, but they can be sublime. At the very least, I'd recommend Beaujolais-Villages.

If, however, you want to go all out in search of spring fever, you could consider whites such as Riesling or even Muscat, with its orangey blossom-like niffs.

Or for the Big Daddy of floral whites, pick a Gewürztraminer. You can find some decent value examples from Chile.

Finally, for simple quaffing to welcome the first rays of springtime, a brilliant place to rummage is Italy – especially if you're after crisp white wines. Think of grape varieties such as Fiano, Falanghina and Verdicchio, all of them offering subtle refreshment, clean and fresh as a sunny spring dawn.

Thinking inside the box when it comes to wine

Since the dawn of time, mankind has found ever more inventive ways to store, ship and pour wine. From amphorae and animal skin flasks to glass and plastics, technology and inventiveness have produced all manner of packaging. And it's amazing how much it matters to us when we buy wine.

There's a stack of modern packaging to choose from – good old-fashioned glass, plastic PET bottles, Tetra Paks and even cans. Have you ever drunk wine from a can? Why should it matter?

But it does. Here's a tip: if you're really upset by how the wine is presented to you, pour it into a glass, toss the packaging away and be happy.

The bag-in-box has got a bit of a bad reputation for being cheap but not necessarily cheerful wine. That may have been true in years gone by, but is it still the case? In Australia, which pioneers an unstuffy approach to wine, the box remains massively popular – not just as a way of serving the good stuff, but also for a variety of post-glugging uses, such as turning the bag into a pillow.

So what are the benefits? For a start, the simplicity. It's super-easy to get at your vino, the box fits snugly in the fridge and you can have a glass or two safe in the knowledge that your wine will stay fresh for between four and six weeks.

Unlike with bottles, you'll never drop and smash one – and being lighter, they are also easier to transport, which means lower carbon emissions. Box wines are invariably for drinking straight away rather than laying down in your cellar, and you should always keep your beady eyes peeled for the sell-by date, as they tend to go downhill after about a year.

The quality is generally at about the party quaffing level rather than anything very much higher, so they're not to be bought if you're aiming to impress the boss/in-laws/bank manager. I reckon this is a pity.

I'm a huge fan of filling your own container to take home from the shop. There used to be a shop in Edinburgh when I lived there that sold wine from the barrel into any container you fancied. I'd love to see a similar project launched in a supermarket, like a filling station for wine.

As far as boxed wines go, if I'm honest, I want to like them more than I do. The potential is there to serve sublime wines in greener packaging that delivers excellence and convenience in every sip. There are couple of recent examples that have given me hope, so perhaps it really is time to start thinking inside the box.

Vive la France! Why the French wine industry is still bursting with life

I'm invigorated. Buzzing, in fact. I've just hopped off a plane after a whistle-stop tasting tour of south-west France, and while there's been much talk recently about French wine plummeting in popularity and needing to up its game to compete with the New World wines, I've just been sampling some of the most terrific wines I've glugged in months.

The country's problem is largely due to the horse-trading, politics and rivalries that prevent regions from working together to really set out their stall and engage wine fans with their wares. But if you can get beyond that, there are some truly special unique and curious wines being produced in the south-west from grapes most of us have never heard of.

Négrette is a great example, with a cherry tang that would appeal to lovers of northern Italian reds such as Barbera and Dolcetto. To find these wines you sometimes have to go off the beaten track or scour restaurant lists for the hidden gems.

I love a blend of Négrette and Syrah, which has a tangy cherry fruit and spicy edge, and works a treat with roast duck or a gamey wild boar banger.

You could also hunt down reds made from Braucol, or whites made from grapes such as Mauzac and Len de l'El from Gaillac – all off the wall, but in a good way. However, on my return to Blighty, I was delighted to find there are a surprising number of wines from this region on the shelves of our high streets.

The most startling moment of my trip was when I took a light aircraft flight over the vineyards – actually, though I say light aircraft, it was more like a lawnmower with a couple of fridge doors for wings. My pilot was Michel, and when he handed control of the plane to me and then jerked the stick so we tumbled around above the vineyards like a pea in a whistle, I can honestly say I giggled and whinnied in a mix of terror and delight.

The flight was highly instructive in showing off the undulating terrain of the vineyards in the south-west, which enables a wide variety of wine styles to be produced – everything from fizz to rosé, dry whites, sweet whites, light reds, the powerful red Malbec-driven wines of Cahors and the butch wines from the Tannat grape found in Madiran.

Diversity aside, there has been a lot of focus on the region due to the suggested health benefits of its reds. Professor Roger Corder's book *The Wine Diet* singles out the chunky reds of south-west France, especially Tannat, linking them to long life and good health. I certainly needed a dose of chunky vino after my sortie with Michel and his aerial japes.

The number of Brits who've settled in the region is startling, with some hilltop villages almost entirely populated with expats. With Toulouse a short flight away, and stunning countryside around the wine producing regions of Cahors, Gaillac, Jurançon and Madiran (as well as historic sites such as Albi Cathedral, which looks more like a fortress than a place of worship), it's an area steeped in intrigue, with stacks of discoveries to be made.

And the wines there are crazy, unique, good value and rewarding!

Will global warming spell the end for your favourite tipples from around the world?

The vineyards are sinking! Well, maybe not quite, but climate change looms large over the industry, with opinions colliding and statistics bent into arguments to support multiple viewpoints. But let's assume for a moment that our vineyards are in danger – what should we be drinking before they vanish altogether?

You might think that marginal climates such as the Champagne region are the frontiers in these weather-beaten times. And they could well be – if the Champagne region heats up, all that fresh zesty ping that makes its fizz so elfish and bright could become sugary and plump, creating a completely different drink.

Of course, English vineyards producing fizz, which tend to be just a few degrees cooler than the Champagne region, could benefit.

According to Greenpeace's document, *Impacts Of Climate Change On Wine In France*, 'We are on a path towards an increase in temperature of four degrees centigrade or even six degrees centigrade between now and 2100. Such a climate scenario would lead to the displacement of vineyards 1,000km beyond their traditional boundaries. At the same time, a large section of traditional vineyards, such as the Mediterranean vineyards, could disappear.'

Put simply, that means we could, in theory, be drinking vino from Glasgow. I recently spoke to one winemaker in France's Burgundy region who complained of rising temperatures, who finds he is increasingly picking early, in September. With a delicate grape variety like Pinot Noir, a rise in temperature could be nothing short of catastrophic.

And it's not just France that's engaging with the prospect of climate change. Australia has been suffering from drought that has clobbered its crop. Livelihoods are on the line – but the Aussies are planning for the future. Already the focus is shifting and there is a buzz developing about regional diversity and cooler regions such as Victoria and Tasmania.

In Chile too I have found winemakers escaping the heat of the Central Valley, venturing high up into the Andes – such as in the vineyards of Elqui valley, where the huge difference in temperature between day and night slows ripening and allows the grapes to retain freshness.

Casablanca is already established as a cool climate region in Chile, defying the heat of the day thanks to a blanket of morning sea mists. You find a similar phenomenon in California's Russian River Valley. In South Africa, winemakers are looking to new regions such as Elim and Elgin for cooler climates.

There is talk of modifying grapes, but climate change may mean not just a rise in temperature but intense and unpredictable weather. There's no doubt we have had freakishly hot years, such as 2003, which gave us the European heatwave (and some impressive reds from England). But then again 2009 is reputed to be one of the greatest vintages in France's Bordeaux, along with 2005 and 2000 in recent years.

A rise in temperature on a global scale could forever change regions such as New Zealand, with its cool climate. Who knows if in the future we'll still be seeing fewer deft, graceful New Zealand wines and more full-on high alcohol whoppers. Or, for that matter, Chateau Inverness! Start the countdown. Time will tell.

Smooth Armada: the amazing variety of wines from Spain's Rioja region

What do you think of whenever you hear the word Rioja? A mellow, easy drinking red wine which matches roast lamb superbly? Bang on. But what else? Well, the Rioja region in northern Spain in fact produces an astonishing range of wines from an amazing array of grapes, soils and climates.

There are three distinct parts: Rioja Alavesa, high up and the coolest, its wines full of zing and freshness; Rioja Alta, slightly warmer, a rich source of bottled finesse; and Rioja Baja, hotter still and lower down – the engine room of the region. These three localities enable Rioja to produce a wealth of styles through blending grape varieties.

And if you think that Rioja just means reds, you're missing out on a huge chunk of the region's riches. You can find whites made from local Viura, Malvasia and Garnacha Blanca grapes that are crisp and zingy, or if you prefer them creamy and rich there's lots to choose from too.

Rosé, or rosado as it's called locally, is also on the up. The red wines of Rioja are founded on the Tempranillo grape, which means 'ripens early'. This versatile variety can become young, fruity, glugging wine, or something more structured for ageing to bring out a more savoury character. Tempranillo is blended with other grapes such as Garnacha (for warmth and spice), Mazuelo (colour and structure) and Graciano, which adds finesse.

With all these varieties at their fingertips, the winemakers of Rioja also decide what style to brew their reds into – and how much to charge. Crianza is a younger style, with one year kept in oak barrels and one year at the winery – they're great for a barbecue or with lamb chops. Reserva wines are the most intensely flavoured, spending three years ageing between barrel and bottle, and with at least one of those in barrel. They are a bit pricier but are cracking with a roast.

Gran Reserva is the daddy, only made in the best years and ageing at least two years in oak barrels and three years in the bottle: awesome with a dose of lamb. You pay quite a price for a decent one, but it's an aged wine that comes to you ready to drink. Unlike some other classic winemaking regions, where you spend a packet on a bottle and then have to lay it down for 20 years, you can crack open your Gran Reserva Rioja straight away when you get home.

The variety of wines in the region mimics the range of food on offer down the famous Calle del Laurel in the local town of Logroño, which serves tapas in a myriad of styles, from local salt cod, piquillo peppers and lamb, to chorizo, jamón and the local cauliflower that's so prized it even has its own appellation.

It's a fab region to visit, but if you can't get out there, the next time you think of sampling a Rioja, break out from your normal choice and taste something more unusual.

Back to the 80s: why Valpolicella is well worth another look

Valpolicella: when did you last order it? In a pizza place in 1983 perhaps? Valpolicella was formerly a badge for cheap plonk that was widely available and we thus felt comfortable ordering. But did we really love it?

My guess is not really. We drank it because it was cheap and we were in a restaurant enjoying simple Italian food – before Pinot Grigio became ubiquitous. Today, what does the name mean?

Valpolicella is a region in northern Italy east of Lake Garda. Its wines tend to be made from the local grapes, headed up with Corvina, sometimes blended with other varieties such as Rondinella and Molinara. Basic Valpolicella is light bodied and can have an off-putting acidity and bitterness, but in better bottles, the cherry-ish tang works brilliantly chilled on a summer day. Valpolicella Superiore is aged for longer and tends to be a bit fuller, higher in alcohol and rounder.

If you see Recioto on the label, it'll be a more structured, sweeter and richer wine produced from partially raisined grapes dried in special rooms called *fruttai*. It may seem weird to make wine from raisined grapes, but consider the difference between a fresh and a sun-dried tomato. The flavours are enriched, more concentrated and tangier.

Ripasso is another style of Valpolicella with a bit of oomph. It's made by adding a young Valpolicella wine to the lees of Amarone during fermentation.

For serious richness, there's only one bad boy to get your chops around: Amarone della Valpolicella. Amarone is similar to Recioto, but made in an off-dry to dry style with a spicy and bitter twang. It tends to be very rich, complex, concentrated and packed with flavour.

But take care. The downside of this wine is the high alcohol content, around 15 per cent, so mind you don't inadvertently tranquillise yourself. It can also be very oaky, which works when in balance with the big, bold fruit, but if overdone can make it feel as dry and unsatisfying as licking a scaffolding plank.

The other problem can be oxidation during the drying, which can lead to an unappealing streak in the final wine. But pick a good example and match it with robust fare such as red meat roasts and you're in for a treat. Amarone also benefits from ageing; it softens up and develops a more savoury character.

Interestingly, while Amarone is one of Italy's better known wines, it's only been awarded the status of DOCG – the highest in Italian wine – relatively recently. Partly this is because consistent quality has only been achieved with more modern air-drying technology. But also, Italian wine legislation is notoriously complex, and change takes a long time.

But will we take it back to our hearts? The price tags for Amarone can be off-putting, ranging from around £15 to several hundred pounds, and in summertime they can be too heavy. But there are lighter styles, and for those who love New World wines such as Aussie Shiraz, Amarone offers the richness of the Old World with the concentration of the New. It's a unique style, a bit like a bear hug from a giant – warm and so powerful it can be a bit terrifying. Be brave!

Shiraz and Syrah are brothers under the skin – same grape, wildly different wines

Shiraz and Syrah are the Ant and Dec of the wine world: although made from the same grape, they are individually unique. Both deliver a robust glass of red vino with a spicy or smoky niff, yet each has a curiously different character.

Broadly speaking, Syrah tends to be from cooler climates, lower in alcohol and has some tangy zip, whereas Shiraz tends to be more fruity and more generously laced with booze, with a right hoof of intense flavour. I love both, so select according to your mood and food. Syrah works with duck, for example, but with Shiraz you need a richer, beefier dish.

Syrah's spiritual home is France's northern Rhône, and in true French style they label the wine by the place, not the grape. So Cornas, Crozes-Hermitage and Côte-Rôtie are all made from Syrah, but each has a different personality. Cornas tends to be inky, meaty and spicy; Crozes-Hermitage can have an amazing aroma of Parma Violets; Côte-Rôtie is classy yet powerful and often includes a squirt of the white grape Viognier to amp up the aromatics.

You've also got Hermitage itself, which can be as savoury as a roll-up cigarette, as chunky as a steak and as fine as a diamond ring. Laying it down for a few years softens up its leathery texture and enhances its complexity.

France also offers some stunning Syrah outside of the Rhône, from regions such as the Languedoc, which stylistically is often friendlier and more modern in a bid to tackle the runaway success which is New World Shiraz.

Shiraz, with its rapid vigour and friendly flavours, can be awesome, and works a treat with a hearty barbie. There are some stonking examples of fine Aussie Shiraz too, which can be stunning – but pricey.

Some countries tackle both Syrah and Shiraz, such as Chile or South Africa.

Meanwhile, across the world, there's a wealth of further styles to choose from. Shiraz rosé offers generous fruit and modern intense colour. You can also find sparkling Shiraz, which, if you haven't tried it, is well worth a punt. Serve it chilled and think of it more as a bramble sorbet than a drink.

But perhaps Syrah/Shiraz's best quality is its talent for getting along with other grapes as part of a blend. It's not just a solo artist, and you can find it in blends of all shapes and sizes, from Australian Shiraz/ Cabernet to French Corbières and Côtes-du-Rhône to Spanish Syrah and 15 Garnacha blends that go perfectly with a slab of hearty beef.

Glug on!

Big name hunters: does a major wine label always mean minor vino?

In the world of wine, there are some big hitters that you can pick up off virtually any supermarket shelf in the UK. We Brits drink big brand names by the bucket.

The genius of these brands is that they remove the perceived risk the consumer takes when selecting wine. They're packaged in a modern way, speak about wine in plain English, and don't try to pretend to be anything other than what they are. But is the wine any good?

Most wine critics will simply answer with a curt 'no'. But I am determined to look more closely at the world of big brands and marketing to better understand why they are so successful.

The big wine brands' key selling point is offering a reliable taste that stays the same. What they have also done is choose a recipe for their style that has one thing in common – sweetness.

Whether you're tasting Sauvignon Blanc or Merlot, most of the big brand wines I tasted felt as though they had been boosted with sugar and then jacked up with acid, like soft drinks.

But beware. There's a danger of amping up inverted wine snobbery by suggesting that somehow these big brands are producing 'fake' wine, that they lack character, that they feel standard, dull and frankly could come from anywhere in the world.

I understand these points, but the fact remains that millions of consumers buy and enjoy the wines made by these well known names. So what should you get?

One tip I can offer is that there are brands out there that may not be the biggest, but they do offer you a reasonable shot at quality and at similar prices to some household names. And amazingly, a huge proportion come from France.

The thing is, the big brands only make the wine they do because we buy them.

The complete summer wine guide:
Part 1

For me, a genius food and drink combination can offer a potent imprint on the mind and unleash a stratum of pleasure that knows no limit. It's all about great food that's good to drink with. When have you ever read that in a restaurant review? I spend my life inventing recipes to match the wild cauldron of flavours that are bursting to get out of my drinks cabinet.

Although the CERN accelerator steals all the hype about particles colliding, the sort of molecular collisions that its scientists rabbit on about occur every day on your plate, in your glass and across your tongue. As soon as you spread butter on to your toast you're effectively breaking and re-making a whole new world of texture, taste and bespoke sensual pleasure.

To make your journey to Flavour Central a little simpler, I've divided my thinking into section headings dictated by flavour, instead of the traditional starters, mains and puddings.

Any two distinct flavours can ignite a spark that blooms and multiplies into a richer dimension of dynamic stimulation. A bit like a horde of miniature carpet bombs firing pleasure and intrigue across your palate. The resulting sense of contrast and delight is capable of eliciting a far more resonant emotional response than the flavours might have done on their own. And, by engaging with place, provenance, newness and the spirit of playfulness, which chefs such as Heston

Blumenthal have deployed to glorious effect, it only gets better.

For me, pairing food with drink is the universe's most immediate and best value holiday. And inventing fresh combinations... well, it's a bit like mining for jewels and discovering a hidden world of limitless horizons on the end of your shovel.

When you combine two flavours that exponentially multiply the deliciousness of the dish, whether it's something as simple as a sip of cognac with a frosty bite of a vanilla ice-cream for a DIY Baileys, or eating a chunk of Stilton with a glass of chilled Hungarian Tokaji, you are making magic.

The point of all these matches, though, is to share them, delight in them and go to bed with a smile on your face that glows, warms and reflects back at you off your ceiling.

Citrus

In wine terms, when you're dealing with lime, lemon, grapefruit or kumquat, the key point to bear in mind is coping with that intense zip of citrus.

The most similar grape variety is Sauvignon Blanc, with its grapefruit-y tang. You can find shrill and elegant Sauvignon Blanc in the Loire Valley, from Sancerre, for example. New Zealand Sauvignon Blanc has become famous for its passion fruit verve, especially the examples from the sunny South Island region of Marlborough.

Meanwhile, South African Sauvignon Blanc has crisp apple characteristics from cooler areas such as Elgin, and even a smoky quality from other plots round the Cape.

How the citrus is deployed in the recipe (for example, whether it is in combination with salty or sweet flavours, rich or fine textures) will have a great impact on the wine style to match it with. When citrus lurks in a creamy, sweet pudding such as a lemon tart, it's usually time to call upon the services of Sauternes – sweet wine from France, featuring the Semillon, Sauvignon Blanc and Muscadelle grapes. These have been dried out and intensified by 'noble rot' – a parasitic fungus that attacks ripe grapes and causes an increase in their sugar content – called Botrytis Cinerea.

The texture of Sauternes is rich and creamy and the acidity is dazzling but there is also a luscious amount of sweetness to balance. Delicious!

Sauternes can be pricey, so if you're after a cheaper alternative, check out wines from nearby Monbazillac – same grapes and a similar style, but less prestigious.

And yet, if there's a citrus streak lurking in a more salty dish, for example something with the briny tang of a green olive, then the nutty and fleshy texture of a crisp, zippy Spanish Fino sherry is called in to play. Forget the stuff your granny drinks: Fino sherry is light, dry and pinging with energy; it's like surfing a crisp wave of outrageous power right up the beach and into the point for a night of revels and ecstasy. Remember to serve it well chilled and keep it in an ice bucket or cooling jacket, and pour into small glasses to maintain that refreshing chill.

Wine with powerfully citrusy dishes such as ceviche – South American citrus-marinated seafood – should complement rather than contrast the dish. We're hunting zing and freshness, so look for white wines produced from cooler climates (think coastal, mountainous or just downright chilly).

From France, Muscadet, Sancerre and Picpoul de Pinet are all worth a shout. In terms of grape varieties, Sauvignon Blanc is a cracker (go to New Zealand for tropical pungency or South Africa for appley freshness), or try Verdelho or dry Riesling from Australia – look for Clare Valley or Tasmania.

But, for me, because I associate ceviche so strongly with Chile, it's got to be a Chilean Sauvignon Blanc – and there are many regions to choose from: Limari, Casablanca, San Antonio and Leyda are my top Chilean regions, producing just the right level of thrust for lift-off with this dish.

If you're really after a citrus explosion, Assyrtiko (you say it 'Ass-ear-tea-ko') is a unique grape variety from the Greek island of Santorini and it gets my vote as one of the best on the planet. It is bone dry and can be packed with the intensity of a lemon harnessed to the thrust of an F-16 fighter jet. Racy, zesty and with a curious salty-smoky tang thanks to the local volcanic soil and the sea mist that creeps over the vines and leaves a little crust of salt on the grape skins. Genius.

One sip usually makes me thirsty for the next.

Sweet

The key when matching a wine to a sweet dish is to make sure that the wine is as sweet as or sweeter than the dish. If your starting point is the sweet wine itself, though, then you don't have to go sweet with your food at all – a glass of Sauternes with a salty chunk of Roquefort cheese is a joyful mouthful.

A wine that works well with treacly flavours, thanks to its dark richness and fortified power, is Australian liqueur Muscat. It's also delicious with fruitcake and any puds that contain dark, dried fruit. It's well worth stocking up for the winter months, to help see you through your cheeky hibernation.

On a more summery note, pour aged Pedro Ximénez over vanilla ice cream and weep with joy. PX is a treacle-black sweet sherry that is super-rich and concentrated – like liquidised figs and dates. It's a real trophy, and an underrated wine from Spain.

Samos sweet wine comes from the Greek island of the same name, and production goes back beyond 1,000 years BC! Made from Muscat à Petit Grains grapes, it's toffee-like and sometimes orangey, along with a luscious sweetness. It works exceptionally well with gingery spice and cinnamon infused puddings.

Now I may sound like a wine pervert, but Italian Moscato d'Asti is the order of the day with white chocolate. The sparkling fizzy elderflower fun of this wine brings a unique counterpoint to the richness of the dessert. And at just eight per cent alcohol, it'll ensure your dinner guests don't slouch into an early, booze fuelled slumber. And, by a happy coincidence, a glass of sparkling Moscato is a rather superb way to start the day, so if there's some leftover then you can have a glass of wine with your breakfast!

Portugal is rightly proud of its port. I'm a big fan of tawny port, which is amber and less heavy than full-on, red, vintage port. I'm especially partial to Tawny port with an age on the label (this is an average age of the wine.) They can be wonderfully concentrated with nutty, caramel and coffee flavours. Serve it chilled with salted almonds as an aperitif on a summery evening and feel the magic.

It is also, in my view, the best style of port to match with Stilton. For a classic British treat, match a digestive biscuit with a Cox's Orange Pippin apple and serve with a glass of vintage port – the best you can find.

Earthy

Things that grow underground or just above it have a wonderful flavour all of their own. Think of mushrooms, but also beetroot's deep purple sweetness, the peppery kick of a radish or the mysterious tang of chard. Certain river fish have an earthy flavour, too – something that makes them unmistakeably 'rivery'. In wine, earthy aromas can be found in older vintages of classy, top notch kit.

In fine, old, red Pinot Noir from Burgundy, for example, it's common to smell a leafy forest floor. In Barolo, there can be truffle-y notes and in red Bordeaux the woody scent of a cigar box is a common description. As a result, aged wine can be a winner with earthy flavours in dishes.

Fava beans are usually what we call broad beans, but in Greece the word refers to split yellow peas – and when they come from Santorini their aromatic, sweet, earthy edge is intense and wonderful. Traditionally they're served with chopped spring onions and olive oil, alongside seared scallops or octopus.

Grown in the same volcanic soil is a zinging white wine also known as Santorini, in which the headline grape is Assyrtiko. This has a superbly bright, dazzling intensity.

With rustic dishes like a hearty bean soup, go for wild wines that glug easily. Places in France like Minervois, Fitou and Corbières offer good value, uncomplicated reds with character and flourishes of spice that would match well. For a dish with herby notes, I love finding wines from south-west France, which are infused with a subtle, herby character from the hillsides known as *garrigue* (think wild thyme and rosemary). Sometimes wines get imbued with the flavours that surround them, you see. There are those who think the earthy, minty aromas in some wines from Australia and Chile come from the eucalyptus and boldo trees growing nearby.

Some swear by Sauvignon Blanc with earthy English asparagus, but I often find it too high in acidity – especially if you're serving the asparagus with butter. I prefer Grüner Veltliner – a speciality of Austria, generally unoaked and with a glassy, cool polish and a grape-fruity twist.

Spicy

Spice adds an extra dimension to a dish. It's like the percussion in a band – it can be a loud marching beat, leading everyone to a climax or a subtler offbeat echo in the background. Spice can operate in two distinct ways: high impact heat or, more subtly, layers of aromatic spice that offer depth of flavour and elegant, expansive qualities to a dish.

It's the difference between adding a chilli or a stick of cinnamon to your curry. They both have a spicy character but in completely different ways. Now that curry is officially Britain's best loved dish, the realm of spice deserves closer attention. Spice in food can clobber your taste buds when it comes to wanting something to drink with it. Generally a chunky red will magnify hot spice in a dish, whereas an off-dry white will taste zingier. Definitely avoid very crisp, dry whites as they will turn into darting, dazzling laser bolts that bounce off your taste buds.

Chenin Blanc from South Africa seems a winner with mild, spicy dishes, from prawns with a sweet chilli dip through to a toasted sesame stir fry. If it's a red you're after, though, go for low tannin with a good fruity flavour.

I've had luck with fruity red Grenache from Australia, especially with curried game such as partridge. In general, Pinot Noir rules the roost with game birds – but if it's really spiced up, Californian Pinot Noir tends to be bigger, fruitier and bolder than its European cousins and with its extra dose of fruit, it's ready to take on the gamiest, spiciest dishes.

With more aromatic spicy dishes, you can go for Gewürztraminer, but I often find its intense floral character and unctuous texture overpowers subtle spice, like a bear strangling a mouse.

When the spice in your dish comes from flavours such as cardamom, cinnamon, ginger and coriander seeds, I would go for Viognier, Chenin Blanc or lesser known varieties such as Marsanne and Roussanne.

All of these have subtle aromatic qualities and, when they have been intelligently oaked, they offer a richness of texture and a superb springboard for a spicy dish.

The complete summer wine guide: Part 2

Creamy

I'm going to start with all things creamy – that's anything from cream teas to the runniest cheese. A dish made with double cream – such as figgy pudding (figs, double cream, Greek yoghurt and brown sugar) – calls for a glass of Sauternes. It has an unctuous texture, glorious sweetness and will manage to cut through the texture of the cream thanks to its brisk acidity.

Or you could grab a Botrytis Semillon from Australia. I also love a glass of Monbazillac, sometimes thought of as the poor relation to Sauternes. It has less acidity, aromas of brioche and a beautiful round-ness that works a treat with custard. And if sweet wine is your thing, check out Muscat from the Greek island of Samos – a gloriously rich dessert wine with an orangey streak.

Now, let's talk about cheese. Generally, if you're dealing with a soft cheese that hasn't got a rind, a white unoaked wine is your target – a crisp English white would do it. (If you're a stickler for reds, head for a lighter style, such as Beaujolais.) The king of soft cheese is Mozza-rella, all creamy freshness and chewy texture – and for that a glass of Prosecco is a sublime match.

With a soft-rind cheese such as Camembert or Brie, go for oaky Chardonnay, South African Chenin Blanc or experiment with Viognier, Marsanne and Roussanne. Smelly cheeses such as Époisses work with spicy rich whites such as Gewürztraminer.

Squidgy cheeses like Port Salut, Reblochon and Pont-l'Évêque work well with Pinot Gris, an underrated variety (it's the same grape as Pinot Grigio but made in a richer style).

The harder the cheese, then the chunkier your wine choice can be. For me, Cheddar cheese is the one occasion that red wine really does comes into play, and Cabernet Sauvignon or even Bordeaux blends are generally a winning combo.

The salty streak of a blue cheese calls for a contrast: think Tokaji or port with your Stilton. Gorgonzola or Roquefort with Sauternes is also worth dosing yourself with. And if you're up for it, bite into a dried apricot with your sliver of blue cheese.

Salty

Salt is vital for creating balance in our daily diet, and when deployed correctly can transform something bland into something with serious potential. And salt doesn't just come from seasoning – think of briny shellfish, green olives, even smoky chorizo... they are all salty in their different ways.

Salt works with crisp, zinging drinks – wines such as Sauvignon Blanc. A glass of champagne with a salty snack is a treat that invigorates the palate with bright, uplifting, cleansing flavours. Fino sherry with green olives or dry Muscadet along with briny oysters are also champion matches. But salt can also work when balanced with a squirt of sweetness, as with salted almonds and Tawny port. Scrummy!

Generally when it comes to the choice of wine, you want to watch out for chunky reds – salt can make them taste bitter so, if you're picking a red, go for lighter wines from grapes such as Gamay, Pinot Noir or Nero d'Avola.

The question of which type of salt to use is one I have asked many chefs and the consensus seems to be Cornish, Welsh or Maldon sea salt, rather than table salt. Smoked salt is a luxury but there are all sorts of other salts, too – I once tried a volcanic salt from Hawaii. And don't forget the library of salty infusers in your kitchen, such as anchovies and soy sauce.

Salt alternatives are one thing, but once you've discovered that a decent dose of salt enhances rather than dominates your dishes, your cooking will flourish.

Salt can be used in a variety of ways to change a dish: instantly by seasoning it; or more gradually, as in the case of curing meat or fish.

And when it comes to fish, the sea is full of noble beasts. As a keen fisherman, I love discovering new fish dishes to prepare. I remember the first time I hauled a red gurnard out of the sea – I half wondered whether I'd caught a magical red flying fish! I remember filming *Saturday Kitchen* with John Wright, the champion forager from River Cottage. His challenge was to produce unusual items of rare culinary appeal for me to match wines to.

I'll never forget the sublime moment he pulled several giant oysters out of his bag – freshly caught in Poole harbour. To my eyes, they were bigger than a human foot. John showed me his technique for shucking them. It felt a bit like busting into Fort Knox, but the oysters inside were simply SENSATIONAL – packed with briny flavour and with an amazing underlying sweetness. They were so massive it was impossible to shuck and eat them whole so we had to slice them into manageable proportions.

So, which wines to choose? Champagne is a classic match with fresh oysters or you could try a New World Chardonnay or Chenin Blanc. Or, if you're feeling posh and flush, a glass of Puligny-Montrachet from Burgundy would be a rocker.

Greek salad is a marvellous jumble of fresh ingredients, herbs and salty feta cheese. A sharp hit of chilled Sauvignon Blanc is fabulous with feta but, if you want to go all out, a Greek Assyrtiko from Santorini, with its salty mineral edge, is a beauty.

The saltiness of Greek dishes such as keftedes works well with a local white wine known as Thalassitis, which means 'from the sea'. The white grapes are irrigated by the salty sea dew, which gives the wine an exceedingly dry edge – chill it down and sip the salt!

Southern Comfort: known for its cheap wines, South Africa is now upping the game

For too long we've thought of South African wine as something simple and friendly to swig at a barbecue. The truth is, South Africa's strength lies in its range of independent minded wine producers and there's also some big brand action to keep the bargain hunters happy.

Stellenbosch is perhaps South Africa's most famous wine producing region. Lots of Bordeaux style blends (wines made from grapes you find in Bordeaux, such as Cabernet Sauvignon and Merlot). But across the Cape, new and invigorating blends become as inventive as Picasso after a pint of absinthe.

I'm thinking of regions such as Swartland, and wines made from several different white grape varieties that manage to be rich yet dazzlingly refreshing.

But South Africa is not just about blends. There's superb sweet wine, sometimes known as 'straw wine'. For an iconic sip, hunt the glory of Vin de Constance from Klein Constantia. Then there's the unique local red wine Pinotage, which some say is like sipping smouldering car tyres but which I say has some fantastic examples. And sometimes – I know it sounds bonkers for a red wine – it can even smell like bananas. A brilliant wine to fox your guests in a blind tasting.

There are classy producers working with Chardonnay – check out the Hemel-En-Aarde Valley, for example. For me though, the runaway success in South African wine is Sauvignon Blanc. You can find a wide range of cracking examples.

For a more fruity glass, target South African Chenin Blanc. It's an outstanding grape variety that comes in a rainbow of flavours from very sweet dessert wine to fresh white wine and even fizz. With its mild aromatic edge, Chenin is a great wine to match with mild curries or even kebabs.

But if it's a hearty red you're after, South Africa has some truly excellent Shiraz (also known as Syrah).

The truth is, the glory of South African wine is only just beginning to kick off.

Nothing gives you a refreshing summer lift like a fine glass of rosé (and yes, it's OK for men to drink it)

Rosé is for girls. Fact. Well, actually, not any more. While it used to be (virtually) the sole preserve of women desiring a sweeter style drink, those days are gone. I'm always amazed when I meet guys who openly mock rosé for being effeminate, but who then leap across a crowded room to get a sip of rosé champagne.

The fact is, rosé now comes in all shapes and sizes – and we're drinking more and more of it. Yes, there are still bottles from big players in the States that seem to taste of melted ice lollies, but there are also plenty of crisper, fresher, drier styles to get your chops round.

Rosé seems to glow in the bottle, and the range of colours available on the supermarket shelves is gobsmacking. When I'm filming *Saturday Kitchen*, my cameraman Jim 'The Captain' Cook often stands me in front of the rosés, as their varying hues stand out more than those of the reds and whites. They go all the way from light to dark – in fact, you can now get rosés so dark they're practically reds. I call these 'butch rosés' and there's no doubt that men feel more comfortable drinking them. They tend to be full of flavour and relatively powerful – you'll find examples from countries such as Chile and Australia.

Other rosés have a Day-Glo pink hue, and others still are so pale they make Scarlett Johansson look tanned – notably the delicate rosés of Provence. (Such is the variety of pale rosés in France that a quest for the palest is the subject of a book, *Extremely Pale Rosé* by Jamie Ivey.) Rioja is a region whose rosé sits somewhere in the middle of the spectrum – fruity but without being too butch, too sweet or too pale.

But rosé shouldn't be judged on looks alone. So many grape varieties go into producing it that it offers an awesome variation in flavours. There's intense rosé made from Syrah, fruity rosé made from Tempranillo and elegant, crisp rosé made from Pinot Noir – for example, Sancerre rosé.

So, how is it made? Well, there are actually three different methods. The first is the *saignée* method, whereby juice is bled off from red wine fermentations. The second involves leaving the red grape skins in contact with the juice, which works rather like dunking a tea bag in a cuppa – the longer you leave the skins in, the deeper the colour. The final, and rarest, method is to blend red and white wine, as is done in the Champagne region.

Rosé champagne is hugely popular, with well known brands to 'prestige cuvées', which cost a stack of loot but can be lush to lick. But don't lose heart: there are also some excellent bottles of rosé cava (or rosado, as it's known locally) to get stuck into, fruity rosé from Italy and top value New World fizz.

For me, there's nothing quite like a cool, frosty glass of rosé for instilling that summertime feeling. Whether you're out on a picnic, lounging in the garden or pondering the drizzle, life just feels more fun when you're in the pink.

Eastern promise: wine's traditional heartlands are being challenged by the vineyards of Croatia, Hungary and Turkey

Gone are the days when Eastern Europe meant a bottle of Bulgarian red plonk – there's some serious vino out there. I once attended the Croatian Chamber of Economy's fine wine tasting in London, and it was fascinating. The tasting featured a host of unique local grapes that hopefully have a future on our shelves.

I sampled the red variety Plavac Mali, the best of which have Zinfandel-like butch flavours and complex spicy richness.

The majority of the Croatian wine producers who showed off their wares don't sell them in the UK, but their attitude was upbeat. Did you know there are 17,000 wine producers in Croatia with 2,500 wines of controlled origin and 200 vine varietals?

Croatian wine has been around for 2,500 years. A statistic that really grabs me is that half the wine produced in the country never reaches the shelves, but is fermented for personal consumption. We're talking about a land of home winemakers. From the Mediterranean to the Alps, Croatia is a thirsty nation – my kind of place.

But for bonkers wine, Croatia isn't the only place you should look. Peer around Eastern Europe and you'll find an increasingly wide range of vino on offer. At the London International Wine Fair, it is astonishing to see the sheer number of insane wines that taste great and come from hitherto under-represented winemaking nations.

Take Turkish wines. I've tasted a few in my time, some good, some bad, but I was knocked out by Narince – a floral zinger of a white variety with an appealing zesty character and mild aromatics similar to scented orange peel.

I've long been a fan of Greek wine, from the vibrant, dazzling whites of Santorini to the reds of Amyndeo. There's a lot more to Greece than retsina.

Hungary too has a long winemaking tradition. I'm a big fan of Tokaji, the famous sweet wine with a lush balance between acidity and sugariness. If you liked Opal Fruits, you'll love Tokaji. But if sweet wine isn't your bag, there are more and more dry wines coming out of Hungary, from floral whites such as Irsai Oliver to mighty reds such as the famous Bull's Blood of Eger.

This summer I'm up for hunting out some newcomers with flavours and textures that can unlock new chapters in our adventures in wine. Let's taste!

How do you keep a shipload of P&O cruisers happy? It's all in the mix...

His eyeballs are hovering over the top of a giant test tube. He pours in another measure of Shiraz, holds the deep red liquid up to the light, sniffs it. Nods. A quiet taste, slurp and then the grin. He hands it to me. 'That, my friend, is the perfect blend.'

I am locked in a lab within a winery witnessing the eureka moment when the proportions of a blend for a wine destined for the UK shelves has just struck.

It's amazing to think that the tiny test tube with an assembly of different grape varieties will be replicated in giant steel tanks before being bottled and shipped to your local supermarket.

Blends are more common than you think. Champagne, for example, can be blended from three principal grape varieties – Chardonnay, Pinot Noir and Pinot Meunier. The idea is that each grape adds something to the mix, such as colour, structure or acidity.

I have created the wine list for *The Glass House* on board P&O's cruise ship, *Azura*. I selected 32 wines from around the world and listed them by style. But one of the biggest challenges was when P&O asked me to select and blend the house wines for the ship.

Blending wine is an art. You need to think about colour, intensity of flavour and the style of wine you want to create – aromatic, zingy, butch, spicy, etc.

There are, of course, traditional blends of grapes such as Cabernet

Sauvignon and Merlot, which form the basis of top French red Bordeaux wines, but there are also highly inventive blends coming out of the New World, refreshing combinations with style and substance.

The bubbly was a bit of a no-brainer – I went for a Prosecco which had winning fruity freshness at the right price.

But for the red, white and rosé, the first question was where to hunt? I tasted wines from as far away as Chile, Portugal, the US and France but it proved tough to find a trilogy from the same winemaker... until I tasted a few samples from Sicily.

Sicily appealed for three reasons: unique local grape varieties, good value wines and the island's location in the Med, within hailing distance of *Azura's* route. We filmed the process of blending the wines and it was a daunting start. Lined up before me were about 50 bottles – and they were just auditioning to be part of the red wine!

The house red is a blend of Shiraz with local Nero d'Avola, which has plenty of deep dark fruit without being too chunky. It appeals to easy drinkers as well as wine aficionados thanks to its quirky blend of famous international grape (Shiraz) with a less familiar variety (Nero d'Avola).

For the white, we settled on a fusion of Pinot Grigio and Chardonnay with a deft crispness and refreshing peachy appeal. The rosé is 100 per cent Cabernet Sauvignon with a generous pinky hue along with candyfloss aromas and summery red fruit flavours.

I'm delighted that the results of my blending debut so far have been very encouraging. The red and the white have both been commended at the Decanter World Wine Awards and all the house wines are now to be released across the entire P&O fleet. Together we have set sail across the high seas of vino.

You can't guarantee clear skies for your barbie, but you can be sure of getting sunshine in a bottle

Just mention the word barbecue to most Brits and they immediately think of rain and scorched meat. But I think we're missing a trick here. With all the sensational flavours that rumble up a storm on the barbie, from prawns to peppers and foil wrapped peaches, there's lots to get excited about. Happily, the same is true for wine.

You're outdoors and – fingers crossed – the sun is shining, so why not polish your tastebuds with a cool, clean glass of Italian white wine or, if you're feeling jazzy, Prosecco. Prosecco appeals to a wide range of palates as it tends to be simple, crisp bubbly with enough fruit to keep you interested but not to distract you from the food.

Another option is to serve green olives, nuts and a selection of cured meats to match a glass of Fino sherry – try an unfiltered Fino for awesome, genius intensity.

Once your guests are sorted with nibbles and aperitifs, you can consider the main event – the blaze!

Barbecues involve smoky flavours, so whites with a jot of oak, proper rosé that's not too sweet, or a medium to light bodied red with a decent whack of fruity flavour all fit the bill. I'd avoid going too heavy on the reds, as not only do they induce sudden bursts of snoozing but they can overwhelm the flavour of a lot of barbecue fare, such as chicken drumsticks and bangers.

For a general red, you're better off with a wine that can be glugged at a stretch. I'm currently a massive fan of southern Italian reds with my BBQ as they match a wide range of foods and aren't so chunky that you need a toothpick to prize out the grapeskins after every sip.

Look for grapes such as Sicilian Nero d'Avola, which you can even dunk in an ice bucket to serve on the chill. For something a bit richer, pick out an Italian Primitivo. Another favourite all rounder is Grenache, especially from Australia, and you could also give French Carignan a go, which reminds me of Pinot Noir's hairier, weightlifting older brother.

You can match lighter red – say Pinot Noir – with meaty fish such as tuna or swordfish. But if it's a fishylicious meal you're cooking, there's a world of white wine out there. Mackerel can work with zinging whites such as Sauvignon Blanc, but with the char of the barbecue I prefer a white Rioja with some oak to flesh out the flavour.

If you're chucking a prawn or two on the barbie, it's an excellent time to get reacquainted with oaked Chardonnay. This can send folk running for the hills – but remember that some of the world's finest white wines are oaked Chardonnays, including Meursault and Corton-Charlemagne.

For a bargain, hunt down Chardonnay from France's Limoux region or have a pop at some of Chile's sexily oaked Chardonnay. Or you could chill down a rosé; for a peachy one with a delicate flavour, splash out on a bottle or two of pink from Provence.

Whichever wine you decide to crack open, remember it's a British summer – so if the sun even thinks about getting his hat on, fire up the coals and target your tastebuds for Barbecue City.

Keep your cool with classic Sauvignon Blanc, and rediscover forgotten gems like Riesling and Muscadet

The first thing that springs to mind when I think of summer whites is refreshment. Arguably the most zinging and crisp grape variety of them all is Sauvignon Blanc – and I adore the stuff.

Sancerre from the Loire is posh Sauvignon Blanc, but for a bargain in a similar style you should look for Sauvignon de Touraine. South Africa and Chile are also both producing good value versions or you might try New Zealand for a more tropical twist – think exotic bright flavours like passion fruit.

For those who find Sauvignon Blanc too sharp, I can warmly recommend an array of Italian whites that are generally crisp without being aggressive. Look for grape varieties like Falanghina and Fiano, or try Verdicchio dei Castelli de Jesi. Another of my current favourites is Greco di Tufo – singing with ping and a great one to stock for summer.

If it's a bargain you're after, hunt for wines that are out of fashion. French Muscadet is a great example of a wine we used to adore but these days is often overlooked. Have another crack at it, especially Muscadet-Sur-Lie, which has a bit more to it. There are some terrific bargains around and if you're munching *moules frites* or shellfish, it's a belter.

Picpoul de Pinet, from the south of France, is a sensationally crisp white wine style that still offers good value. There's also Vinho Verde from Portugal or even Txakoli (you say it 'chakolee') from northern Spain – a light zesty white that's low in alcohol so is perfect for lunch-time.

German whites remain underrated and a cool refreshing glass of dry Riesling Kabinett is, for me, a winner. Riesling from Australia's Clare Valley is more fashionable and makes a fab summer sipper with its lime freshness and spankingly gorgeous aroma of tangerines.

Another way to tackle your planning for summer white wine nirvana is to break out and replace your regular tipple with a white wine of a similar style. Spanish Albariño, for instance, usually appeals to lovers of dry whites such as Chablis, while fizz from France's Limoux can be a winner instead of Champagne.

In fact, for summer whites, value fizz is a great way to go – Spanish cava can be stonking value; Italian Prosecco is fun on its own or mixed with fruit juices – peach purée, for example.

If you prefer wines with a more aromatic kick, get your chops around Argentinian Torrontés – bright and lemony with stacks of floral fun.

But if it's refreshment you're after as well as a food match, grab a zinging bottle of Sauvignon Blanc and serve with chunks of goat's cheese before dinner – a glorious way to enjoy a cracking dose of summery white wine.

Should you always drink white wine with fish? Or is this one rule that's made to be broken...

I'm hurtling through the streets of London in a taxi driven by Dave. He used to be a fishmonger and he only ever drinks white wine. Blimey, he's taking the white wine with fish rule to the max! But in truth you can match a flotilla of wine styles to fish.

Think about the range of fishy flavours and textures: light and oily mackerel, meaty and chunky monkfish, sea fish, freshwater fish, shellfish, smoked fish and then hundreds of ways to cook and prepare our fishylicious hoard. This is great news for wine lovers because the world's your oyster.

For an oily fish like mackerel, try whites with zesty fresh acidity to cut through the texture – Sauvignon Blanc or English whites can be very successful. With similarly oily fish such as sardines, bright fresh wines such as Portuguese Vinho Verde are highly refreshing.

How the fish is prepared counts for a great deal. If you think about very pure fresh fish flavours like sashimi they tend to be mild and clean, and rarely 'fishy'. For these deft banquets I'd stick to Italian whites, and grape varieties such as Verdicchio hit the spot with their unoaked freshness and purity.

But when you start to cure, smoke, bake or fry fish, subtle differences come in to play with texture and intensity. Always think about the dominant flavour in the dish. A steamed fillet will taste far less intense than one curried in a spicy sauce.

When you are browning a fish in a pan and getting the skin nice and crispy, there are toasty flavours there that call for white with an oaky edge. You could experiment with lightly oaked white Rhône wines blended from grapes such as Marsanne and Roussanne. Similarly, with smoked fish, a dose of oak goes a long way to stand up to the pungency of flavour. Smoked haddock goes well with a rich oaky Chardonnay from South Africa, California or New Zealand.

Muscadet from northern France's Loire is an amazing wine to match with fish thanks to its unique salty tang (think sea breeze freshness). It can offer terrific value for money and matched with a plate of mussels simply cooked as in *moules marinières*, you can attain flavour nirvana for the price of a cinema ticket.

If you're cooking up a fishy plate of bouillabaisse stew, try southern France's answer to Muscadet, Picpoul de Pinet, a wonderfully refreshing zinger.

Shellfish offers a world of joy for wine lovers: scallops with Grüner Veltliner, crab with Viognier, lobster with Champagne (or Spanish cava for a bargain) and then the humble prawn. I reckon the prawn tossed in garlic butter, flambéed in Cointreau or grilled on the barbecue calls out for a top class glass of Chardonnay – zingy, cool and with a peachy twist of oak to flesh out the mix.

As for meaty fish such as monkfish, tuna or swordfish, you could try lighter reds such as Pinot Noir, Beaujolais, or even Sicilian Nero d'Avola. I've even been served red mullet matched with Blaufränkisch, which was a surprisingly successful match. But what of turbot, the king of fish?

For me, Viognier is the grape to crown it with, in particular, Condrieu from France. But remember, just like Dave the taxi driver, by all means stick to what you love but remember occasionally to cast your net that little bit wider.

How very neat – we're awash with gin that's fit to be drunk straight up

Why don't we drink more gin straight up? We happily glug other drinks such as bourbon and tequila neat or on the rocks. Gin is a fab drink laced with intriguingly refreshing flavours, and I'm a fan of embracing its glorious purity with perhaps just a splash of water or with a splosh of Martini.

I guess partly this is in reaction to the lack of top notch mixers on the market. Happily, spirits such as gin are being set free by a wider range of serious quality mixers. But there's far more to gin than the ubiquitous G&T.

Let's begin with the basics. For starters, no two gins are alike. Broadly, you can divide them up into London gin, which is very dry, Plymouth Gin, which tends to be a touch more fruity, and what I term 'novelty gins', which have a quirky headline ingredient.

Juniper is always the dominant flavour, but the other botanicals can vary hugely: think star anise, orris root, angelica, citrus peel, cardamom and so on.

Then there are those gins that have made a virtue of particular ingredients, such as cucumber or geranium.

There are gins for different occasions. If you want a jot more sweetness, Plymouth Gin is a good one to hunt. London gin is where most of the classy dry gins are at.

Bring on the summer of gin!

The Eighties are back – and so is northern France's favourite white, Muscadet

Muscadet is out of fashion. For the discerning drinker, this is excellent news – because it's cheap. Once, it was the tipple of choice – in the Eighties we swilled the stuff like it was the essence of nectar. Today, we walk down the supermarket aisles and dare not mention its name. What went wrong?

In part, I think we got too familiar with it, but I also think quality could have been less patchy. Thankfully, there's been significant invest-ment in Muscadet so that today's bottle offers some decent value to those in the know. And the really splendid part is that it often tastes far better than you remember it.

So what exactly is Muscadet? It comes from north-west France, in the Loire region. It's made from the Melon de Bourgogne grape (which is sometimes known simply as Muscadet) and pairs exceptionally well with shellfish. *Moules marinières* and Muscadet is as sublime a match as Jayne Torvill and Christopher Dean in the midst of Boléro.

Why? Muscadet has a briny, ever so slightly salty tang to it – which I absolutely adore, as no matter how chilled I serve it, it always makes me thirsty for another sip. My kind of wine.

And if talk of a salty edge to your glass of vino is putting you off, think again – it's like the freshness of an invigorating ocean breeze cooling your very essence on a hot day.

It's not just a winner with mussels either. With oysters it's a bargain alternative to champagne, and it also works with a surprising number of fish dishes, such as sardines, as well as beurre-blanc and brown butter sauces.

However, for me, Muscadet is what an aperitif is all about. If you're the kind of person who loves a dry Martini, or who has sipped Fino sherry and felt the hand of destiny beckon them for another glass, then this wine should be at the top of your shopping list.

Muscadet comes from some of Brittany's only vineyards, with some of the better quality examples hailing from the Sèvre-et-Maine area – this should be clearly labelled on the bottle. Look out for 'Sur Lie' on the label, too, as that's a good thing for adding a layer of complexity to your vino – the wine stays in tanks over the winter on its lees (dead yeast cells), which fleshes out the body and gives it a satisfying tang.

That's what you should be after – especially if you're matching it with food. The danger with bog standard Muscadet is that it's a touch, well, dull. In the wrong hands, the Melon de Bourgogne grape can become as boring as licking cling film. But when it's given the right treatment, it produces a wine that's so fresh it makes the Atlantic Ocean look like a muddy puddle.

I could swill the stuff all day long – and happily it remains one of the best bargains on the shelves. But if you've never had it, how do you know if you'll like it?

Well, if you're somebody who enjoys the flavour of dry wines such as Sauvignon Blanc and salty snacks such as green olives, and loves the smell of the seaside, then this is the perfect wine for you.

However, if your penchant is for sweet rosé and you're someone who can't snack on a fresh strawberry unless it's laced in sugar, Muscadet may send you running for the hills.

The good news for fans of the wine is that it's not the only hidden gem tucked away on the supermarket shelves. The northern French are rightly proud of their fresh, tingly Muscadet, but the southern French have a delightful riposte: Picpoul de Pinet. It's what they match with their *bouillabaisse* fish stews, and sip as an aperitif under the cypress trees before thrashing the next village at boules, then going on strike for a week because the weather's nice.

With cream or on their own, they're the taste of summer – so which wines go best with strawberries?

The British summer is awash with strawberries. We cram them in by the bucketload: at Wimbledon alone we consume around 30 tons, and most of us will at least consider ravaging a PYO farm at some stage during the season – nothing tastes quite as awesome as a freshly picked berry. Refreshingly sweet flavour, squishy texture and the zing in the tail make you yearn for the next bite.

I find strawberries highly addictive and adore them in jams, tarts and ice-cream – but if I'm truly honest I love nothing more than a fresh strawberry in its naked state. When they're perfectly ripe, there's no better emblem of summer. But given the extent to which we worship their god-like flavour, what on earth should we be drinking with them?

Now, you may immediately think of Pimm's, and that's a good shout. Strawberries in the mix with Pimm's is fab, and I'm a well known worshipper of Mr Pimm. But get this: have you ever tried adding chopped strawberries to a jug of chilled white wine?

It's a trick that the camera crew used to use when I was away filming *Cheers From Chile* in South America. If they had a white wine that was crisp, dry and neutral, they'd chop some fresh strawberries and bung them in the jug – even adding ice on a hot day.

Now, I'm not saying that every wine is suitable for this, but if you think about it, it's not a million miles from adding a fruit purée to your glass of Prosecco or boosting your fizz with blackcurrant cordial to make a Kir Royale. Strawberries tossed into a jug of simple chilled white wine, or even a slice of strawberry in a glass of good value fizz such as Prosecco, can bring a sense of occasion and summery fun to your day.

But wait for it. There are those who consider that serving a bowl of strawberries steeped in red wine such as a hearty Shiraz and then grinding fresh pepper over the top is flavour nirvana. It's not the most obvious combo, so try it on a small scale to see if you like it (it tends to evoke a fairly clear cut Marmite type love-it-or-hate-it response). Half a strawberry sprinkled in pepper in a dessertspoon of red should give you the heads up.

At the super-posh end of the scale, I've seen fans of strawberries and top red wine splash out on a pricey bottle of Margaux just to slosh over their fruit. For me, that's taking things a touch too far. Don't get me wrong, I love them both – but for fruit-sloshing, I'm opening the everyday red vino! And if I'm ever lucky enough to taste top-level Margaux, I love getting to know the hidden layers of the wine without altering its flavours.

For me, a major factor in matching wine with strawberries is what you're serving the little red morsels of glory with. Often with food, matching the dominant flavour of the dish can lead to a surprising wine choice. For example, when you serve strawberries with cream, there's a richer, thicker texture to consider, and a mellowing flavour to think about when selecting a wine.

For this kind of classic combo, a richly layered pudding wine is perfect. Late harvest Jurançon is an option, or sweet wines from the Loire such as sweet Vouvray or Bonnezeaux, both made from the Chenin Blanc grape.

I guess the most famous sweet wine is Sauternes from Bordeaux, made from Semillon, Sauvignon and Muscadelle grapes infected with 'noble rot'. It sounds foul, but it concentrates sweetness and acidity in the grapes – if you're a fan of Opal Fruits or sweet-and-sour sauce, you'll probably dig Sauternes.

And with strawberries and cream, it's a wonder. However, it costs a fair old stash of cash, so it's not a bad idea to look for supermarket own label versions or cunning alternatives such as Botrytis Semillon from Australia, or Monbazillac, which comes from near Sauternes and is similarly sweet while tending to command lower prices.

But for superb value, crack open a bottle of sweet bubbly Moscato – Asti Spumante is the sort of stuff. Chill it out, pop the cork and revel in its sweet frothy fun – it's like liquid sherbet and superb with sweet strawberries. Now then, where's my hammock?

Don't limit yourself to white and rosé when the weather's warm – sip some chilled reds

Summer and red wine can be a tricky nut to crack. On a balmy day, the very scent of a barbecue triggers a deep instinct within me to vault over the nearest garden fence to quell my craving for charred meat. But what to sip on such a glorious occasion?

Chilled whites can be lip-smacking and thirst quenching, rosé could be the ticket with its instant summery appeal, but you might be tempted to dismiss reds as being too heavy, too rich and altogether too much.

Think again. There's a whole breed of red wines with a lighter body and a fruity angle that are perfectly suited to being lightly chilled in an ice bucket or the fridge (if it's hot, your wine will warm up in the glass, so it's wise to keep an ice bucket close to hand). If you can't quite get your head around it, just think of them as butch rosé, or imagine a lamb chop gently sizzling on the barbecue just waiting for a glass of refreshing red – a meatylicious match.

But before you start grabbing all the red wines you can, gleefully hurling them into barrels of ice, let's deal with the basics. Not all reds are suitable for chilling. Reds that are aged, savoury or very rich in body are generally not suitable. Tawny port is a notable exception, but we'll come to that.

What you're ideally after are young reds that have a fruity character without being too chunky.

France is awash with such styles of wine. Consider Gamay, a light and fruity grape that produces wines that can be brilliant served chilled. Gamay is the grape variety behind Beaujolais, a style of wine we used to adore – remember the rush for Beaujolais Nouveau? Summer is the perfect time to reacquaint yourself with this lighter style of red and give it a whirl after chilling it in the fridge, much as you would with a white wine.

At the finer end of Beaujolais, with the so called 'cru' wines such as Fleurie and Morgon, you can find more structure, depth and tannin; but you can still experiment with some light chilling. If you see Beaujolais-Villages on the label, it's a step up from basic Beaujolais, but not as prestigious as the 'cru' level – generally featuring good fruit and one to consider chilling.

Another of my favourite areas of France for chillable reds is the Loire. Cabernet Franc is the grape variety to nab, and these wines can have a degree of richness and structure, but just on the right side to make them suitable for chilling – magnificent with meaty fare. Look for examples from places such as Saumur-Champigny and Chinon. They tend to have quite dark fruit with a satisfying tang to it, and with a cold roast beef sandwich outdoors can make you wonder whether all red wine could work chilled. It doesn't, of course, but you're not limited in your experimentations.

A bottle of Pinot Noir from Chile can be delish after a dunk in an ice bath, and you can even try cooling down fruity Grenache based wines. And the fun doesn't stop there. Ever tried sparkling Shiraz from Australia?

Fizzy red wine may sound utterly bizarre, but think of it as more like a cold bramble sorbet and you'll get on a lot better with it. The Aussies often serve it with turkey and trimmings at Christmas when the weather Down Under is piping hot, and it works a treat.

I've been served very young Rioja cool (look for 'Joven' on the label), and even Blaufränkisch. But the far north and south of Italy come up trumps for me, with Dolcetto in the north and Nero d'Avola in the south. With fine structure and summery, fruity appeal, it works brilliantly after a spell in the fridge.

Finally, we come to the rule breaker – Tawny port. It's an aged style of port with a nutty colour and an awesome dried fruit flavour (think raisins and sultanas, even nuts), and it works a treat served well chilled as an aperitif with a bowl of salted almonds.

If you can find it, Colheita is a tawny port from a single vintage and makes a smashing treat to kick off a day of sipping in the sunshine.

Glorious!

Don't pop the budget on pricey vintage fizz
– you can find crackling bubbly for under £10

Popping a bottle of fizz is the ultimate sound effect. It signifies that the good times are rolling, the party is starting and there's serious celebrating to be done. But let's be honest: regular blasts of bubbly can take quite a toll on your wallet – especially if you develop a taste for the really top end stuff.

So how do you maximise value but still enjoy the champagne lifestyle? Well, you could always drink less of it, but life without bubbles can be like life without sunshine: it's OK for a bit, but we all thrive on an invigorating dose now and again. So rather than curtail your love of bubbles, you're better off having your cake and eating it... by being in the know.

If it's champagne you must have, then be aware of the different levels and cost implications. The 'prestige cuvées' are some of the priciest, with famous names sometimes setting you back upwards of £100.

These are generally only made in exceptional years and from the very first pressings of the very best grapes from Champagne's most tip-top sites.

Next up is vintage champagne, which is made from a single grape harvest and can cost over £30 for name brands. But if you buy supermarket own label the prices are more like £20, and the quality is often superb.

Then, of course, you've got non vintage champagne, which is blended from grapes from different years and offers a certain amount of value, especially if you buy from smaller producers and co-operatives. But if you're aiming for well under a tenner, you'll have to accept that champagne may have to come off your shopping list.

Thankfully you can enjoy a similar drink made in the same method simply by looking elsewhere in France. Look for 'Crémant' on the label: generally under a tenner, it's similar to champagne, though arguably with less finesse.

The Loire produces some good examples, and you can find some Burgundian ones too – even Alsace is at it. But for me Limoux is the place in France to hunt for a brilliant bargain bubbly.

France aside, Spain offers a lot of fizz for your buck – cava is made using the same traditional method as champagne but with local Spanish grapes. There are reliable brands, but you can also find outstanding value among the supermarket own labels.

There's also some serious value to be obtained from outside Europe. New Zealand has some excellent examples of bottle fermented sparkling wine, though the price tags are generally above the £10 hurdle.

Australia has plenty to offer, too – quality fizz from Tasmania that costs a bit more (but can be smashing) and endless examples of big brand bubbly for under a tenner.

With 'traditional method' bottle fermented bubbly, each bottle is individually dealt with to ensure the quality is superb – fine tiny bubbles and plenty of them. But there are also methods that are cheaper, if less fine, such as the 'tank method', whereby the secondary fermentation occurs in a giant tank rather than individual bottles. The bubbles tend to be harsher and may conk out quicker, but if it's a quick hit of bubbly you're after, this could be one to try.

For me, though, it's finding proper fizz for under a tenner that makes the heart leap. Some champagne houses make fizz in California, and you can find several good examples coming out of South Africa too. Hop in the bubbly wagon and don't spare the horses!

With an all-star line up, Spanish wines are more than a match for anyone

The Spanish are celebrating in a style that makes me want to emigrate – because their wines have never tasted better.

Spain is a marvellous hotbed of contradictions wine wise, producing everything from sherry in the far south to Rioja in the north. But you probably don't realise just how big a player Spain is in the world of wine. With 1.2 million hectares of vines – around 15 per cent of the world's total – it boasts the largest area of cultivation on the planet.

It's hardly surprising there's a Spanish wine style for all seasons. And thanks to its quirky blends, emerging regions and a run of successful recent vintages, there's never been a better time to tuck into some tapas and raise a glass of something to make your spirit shout 'Olé!'

Let's start with cava – usually thought of as a bargain bubbly. Cava is made via the same traditional method as champagne, with each bottle going through secondary fermentation, resulting in finesse and quality pinhead bubbles. With fizz, the smaller and more delicate the bubbles the better. Cava can deliver this, and in my view you're missing a trick to think of it as a straight swap for Champagne.

Cava tastes unique thanks to the use of local grape varieties, Macabeo, Parellada and Xarel-lo. The crisp apple-y lemony flavour and softer, more scented rosados (rosé) make for a world of exploration.

If you're after young, fresh wines, Albariño from Galicia is one of my favourite summer tipples, a white that works a treat with shellfish

– one to pour for fans of bone dry vino such as Chablis. Wines from Rueda will also quench your thirst for dry whites.

Spain is rightly famous for its reds. José Pizarro, the godfather of Spanish cuisine in Britain, is passionate about the connection between Spanish food and red wine. 'I love Extremadura, near where I grew up. Its signature red goes beautifully with rich meats and cheeses – the heart of every Spanish meal – and with lamb it's simply sensational'.

Naturally, there are accolades aplenty for red Riojas, which range from fruity styles (look for 'Joven' on the label) through Crianza (aged for at least one year in the barrel and one in the bottle) and rich Reserva (one year in the barrel and two in the bottle) to more savoury Gran Reserva (two years in the barrel and three in the bottle). There are also zingy or creamy, rich white Riojas and rosé Riojas. If you're a fan, you should check out the wines of Ribera del Duero, which are based on the same Tempranillo grape and can attain serious richness and savoury complexity in the hands of iconic producers.

And the fun doesn't stop there. Priorat is a region producing outstanding red blends that can attain a silky mineral richness thanks to the llicorella soil, which forces the vines to stretch out deep in search of water. Think of them as like athletes – the more they stretch and train, the more charged their performance.

For a lighter, more summery red, check out wines made from the tangy and lighter bodied Mencia grape, from places such as Bierzo. It's a must for any fans of Beaujolais and Pinot Noir.

In many respects, though, the glory of Spain is in its simple combinations of food and local wine. A glass of well chilled Fino or Manzanilla with jamón, green olives and Manchego cheese remains one of my favourite ways to spend a warm evening. But perhaps the most glorious Spanish combination of all is the most irreverent – pouring thick, treacly Pedro Ximénez sherry over vanilla ice cream for pudding.

Try an award-winning wine for less than £10

I love the awards season. In the wine trade we have various different awards ceremonies and dinners throughout the year and it's not just big name producers that win the gongs, as they often go to wines that are amazing value and from unexpected places.

That's what I really love about awards – they throw up unexpected results and it's all about the kit in the bottle. The wines are tasted blind, so brands, flash labels and packaging are irrelevant. It's all about the quality of the wine.

We've got several awards in this country. I've judged for the International Wine Challenge and the Decanter World Wine Awards and I've even been awarded a gong myself by the International Wine And Spirits competition as Communicator Of The Year.

Generally you'll get wines that achieve bronze, silver or gold medals together with trophies and special awards. A gold medal really matters – believe me. I've judged for days on end and when a really stonking wine gets unleashed, the buzz is palpable and it's a massive achievement for a winemaker.

Silver and bronze also count, and the true glory of these awards is that they range across every wine style you can imagine. If you see a sticker on a bottle in a supermarket carrying an award, generally it's a good way of taking the risk out of buying your bottle of vino. More than that, if you're someone who adores a particular style of wine, you can zero in on a particular trophy to ensure you get the best bottle possible.

Small producers doubtless benefit from awards, but it's right and fair that when big brands get it right the accolades are forthcoming.

It's also good news that the awards suit all pockets. There are plenty of belting award-winning wines out there for less than £10 in the supermarkets.

Value aside, awards also give tribute to ambassadors of particular countries and regions that really show off potential and innovation – and this is where the sweet spot of buying by awards comes into its own.

You can splash the cash on these wines safe in the knowledge that they've been tasted by a panel of people whose life revolves around wine – they're taking the risk out of your purchase and giving you the green light to try something new, different and exciting. Go on, go for gold.

When the evenings are drawing in but there's still time to enjoy the last of the summer wine

Growing up, there was a house next door to my school called 'Finella'. Every autumn, as the summer holidays went into exile for another year, I'd be faced with that name, and with it a sinking feeling as though my heart had turned into a cold jelly.

For me, that intangible, dreaded back-to-school feeling became privately known as 'Finella'. I've never told a soul until now. Who knows, perhaps it'll catch on.

As I write this, I have just returned from my summer holidays and am delighted to say that I haven't the slightest feeling of Finella. In fact, quite the reverse: I've had a spiffing time staying by the Helford River in Cornwall and here I am back tasting wine.

Still, I appreciate that I am a very lucky chap, and in the spirit of quashing that here-comes-autumn feeling across the nation, this column is dedicated to bargain wine guaranteed to make you feel a little less back-to-school and a little more last-of-the-summer-wine.

I'm a believer in Sicily for good value, with local red grapes such as Nero d'Avola and whites such as Grecanico and Fiano offering characterful value for money.

Spain can sometimes do the business too, with bubbly cava, whites from Rueda and sherry. I guess the old maxim of buying out of fashion also counts, but bear in mind some wines are out of fashion because of the way they taste – you may not like them.

That said, I can't resist a crisp glass of Muscadet to match with moules or oysters, or indeed as a terrific aperitif. For me, it remains underrated and a brilliant alternative to fresh white wines such as Pinot Grigio and Sauvignon Blanc.

In days gone by, Down Under provided a source of wines that offered terrific value for money, as well as brands whose wines offered consistent flavours year in, year out. However, after droughts, fires and economic crunching, Australia is a better place today to look for rising quality wines with a real sense of personality.

Whether it's Shiraz from the Barossa Valley, Riesling from Clare Valley, Cabernet Sauvignon from Coonawarra, Pinot Noir from Victoria, bubbly from Tasmania or classy wines with elegance and finesse from Margaret River, Australia is shifting into a place where value is still happening, but quality at the right price is rising up the agenda.

In the New World, Chile has been producing wines that punch above their weight for a while, but I've seen one or two bargain basement offerings of late, including some supermarket own label disappointments that to me threaten to devalue the perceived rising quality of Chilean wine.

Where Chile is concerned, of course you can find wines under a fiver but for me I'd buy smarter for around six quid and actually enjoy drinking the stuff.

France has received a bit of a hammering of late due to its bureaucracy and prices, but I'm happy to say that the nation that regards itself as the home of wine is producing some good kit at impressive prices.

In the main this is the Vin de Pays / IGP category, where winemakers have a bit more freedom to make wines in a style that can compete with other markets such as the New World but also maintain a sense of local character.

Supermarkets are offering us value in these uncertain economic times but beware, sometimes cheap wine is just cheap.

Whichever way your budget leads you, just be sure that you quash that back-to-school feeling and put a finish to Finella once and for all.

As our orchards burst with fruit, it's time to rediscover Britain's finest ciders and perries

The season of mellow fruitfulness is upon us! I love the time of year when Olly HQ is filled with the smell of jam on the brew, chutney on the simmer and the apples are so plentiful they're practically rolling in from the garden shouting, 'Eat me, brew me, crush me!' Apples and pears are a significant part of Britain's heritage and until a few years ago it seemed that cider and perry were perilously close to disappearing from our shelves and bars for good.

Then came the marketing idea of serving cider on ice, and suddenly the boom from the orchard could be heard rumbling in the darkest corners of our cities. No longer was it a drink for scruffy wurzels – cider and perry had been to the barbers and had a makeover.

I've been tasting a wide range of samples and there are a number of ways to categorise cider and perry.

Is it from a single vintage? Is it a novelty brew blended with other fruits? What type of apple is it made from? And is it any good?

Just as you have different grape varieties that influence the taste of wine, so you have hundreds of cider apple varieties, such as Foxwhelp, Brown Snout and Chisel Jersey, each with different levels of bitterness, sharpness and sweetness that contribute to the final brew. Orchards, like vineyards, behave differently depending on local conditions, each one with its own unique influences of climate, rainfall, yield and typicity.

At the National Collection of Cider & Perry at Middle Farm, Lewes, Sussex, the collection on taste is fantastic – cider and perry from up and down the country, all to taste or take home. You can 'sample every pomoligical product and toast the unparalleled quality of our orchard treasures'.

If you want to learn more about British cider, check out cideruk. com the website of the National Association of Cider Makers. It tells you everything you need know about how cider is made, its history and quirky facts. For example, in 1664 John Evelyn wrote: 'Generally all strong and pleasant cider excites and cleanses the Stomach, strengthens Digestion, and infallibly frees the Kidneys and Bladder from breeding the Gravel Stone'. What a helpful chap.

But what of the ciders themselves? Well, there seems to be a sharp demarcation between the mass produced, readily available kit and the local farm brews, with some fine producers somewhere in between. On the whole the standard is good and in comparison to other drinks there's some great value on offer.

To be honest, I'm not a big fan of dosing cider with other fruits – for me it takes away the appleyness of the whole drink.

Perhaps the most perplexing bottles were the low alcohol ciders. With just 0.5 per cent alcohol and disappointing flavour – why not just buy apple juice, sparkling or still, and boost it with a trickle of real cider for a superior taste?

Gripes aside, there's a world of brews out there, from everyday big names to supermarket own labels.

It's great news for British cider drinkers, as Aspall's Henry Chevallier Guild told me: 'The apple may have travelled all the way from Kazakhstan over time, but it seems to have made its natural home in Britain; the richness and diversity of the varieties that have been propagated here in the past three centuries gives cider makers a pool of raw material even broader than winemakers have access to. We need to celebrate what was once our national drink more than we do.'

Drink up, it's harvest time!

Chile's geographical diversity is reflected in its variety of wines – from bargain sipper to boutique bottle

I once spent a magnificent few months filming a show for Chilean television called *Descorchando Chile* (or *Cheers From Chile* in its English version). I learned many things while I was there.

Firstly, if you have blond hair and are filming with an alpaca, the alpaca will definitely try to eat your hair, mistaking it for a hay bale.

Second, the Pollito spider won't bite you, even though it looks massive, has legs like a hairy horse and loves nothing more than climbing up your leg during breaks from filming.

Third, it's completely safe to go disco dancing in the remote town of Talca, even when the DJ points at you and yells that you're 'the albino Latino' so that everyone turns and goggles at your futile attempts to salsa.

Wine wise, the news is even better. Chile remains one of my favourite wine producing countries.

The thing about Chile is that it's incredibly geographically diverse: a long, thin nation that rises up from the Antarctic through lush valleys and arid deserts, it's bordered to the west by the cool waters of the Pacific and on the east by the Andes. What this means is that it offers incredibly diverse virgin landscapes that are potentially suitable for all kinds of grape varieties, from Riesling to Malbec.

Traditionally, the Central Valley has been something of an engine room for Chile, pumping out wines such as Cabernet Sauvignon and Merlot, offering excellent value. But to me, value is just one aspect of the country's success story. What we really need to understand is that Chile has the potential to become one of the most fascinating, daring and engaging wine nations in the world.

The wines I tasted in more marginal regions, such as coastal San Antonio or in the Elqui valley in the Andes, successfully managed to balance the outstanding levels of sunshine with a cooling climatic influence, resulting in a ripeness and natural freshness that I adored.

The rewards for adventurous and experimental winemakers can be massive. They spend their lives driving up and down the length of the country hunting out small and unique vineyard sites, sometimes with old vines (which, it's suggested, impart concentration and complexity) and sometimes new locations that push the boundaries in an inspirational way. Such risk taking potentially opens up new horizons for Chilean wines, helping them stand out on the crowded UK wine shelves. And although, like most wine regions, it's not entirely pest free, it is free from the vine pest phylloxera.

The two grape varieties that stood out for me were Sauvignon Blanc and Syrah – though that's not to say Chile isn't capable of producing outstanding wines from other grapes such as Chardonnay. There are some improving examples of Pinot Noir, too. Meanwhile, if you're a fan of Shiraz you should definitely get your chops round Carmenère; with its deep peppery spice and chocolatey flavour when oaked, it's a great match with a beefy steak.

What excites me most about Chilean wine, though, is innovation. I'd love to see more Mediterranean sun-worshipping red grape varieties such as Touriga Nacional planted, for example. And some winemakers are creating wild and marvellous blends.

The country boasts some incredible winemaking talent – think of big names harnessing big winemaking talents. It's right that winemakers are achieving status and repute when their wines are consistent and excellent. My vote goes to Elqui valley for a fix of meaty, spicy Shiraz

Chile may be over 200 years old, but its wine trade seems to be experiencing a youthful creative spurt. Cheers – and viva Chile!

Hermit Crab? Cat's Pee? You can't judge a wine by the label, especially if it has a funny name

We all remember wines with standout names such as Fat Bastard and Cat's Pee On A Gooseberry Bush, but in recent years, the penchant for wines with quirky names appears to have dwindled. Or has it?

I'm less wowed by wines with names that play on sex, double meanings or just plain coarseness, but the truth is, it's what's in the bottle that counts.

I reckon a lot of wine buyers are put off by many wines that are labelled in languages which are hard to pronounce and with no plain English facts to indicate what might be in the bottle.

I love drinking Aghiorghitko from Greece – a red wine that has a beautiful round richness that would appeal to fans of Shiraz. But it's tricky for a lot of people to say. If I told you that the name Aghiorghitko actually translates as 'St George', it might be less of a big deal for you to get involved with.

It has to be said that sometimes wine labelling can be maddening when it comes to making wine accessible. At the same time, there are exciting traditions in wine that link certain styles to certain places – for example, the fragrant and delicious Sicilian red from the DOCG of Cerasuolo di Vittoria.

But does this tell you anything about the wine at all? Probably not, but by the same token, I would suggest you could learn just as little about a wine that's got a catchy name purely for the sound of it – for example, Cleavage Creek. What grapes could that be, what might it taste like?

Sometimes there's no more information in a catchy sounding name than in the maze of the appellation system (the legally defined and protected indication used to identify where grapes are grown). But at least the appellation system has a set of rules you can research.

But let's be honest, you're more likely to remember a wine with a name like Cardinal Zin than Grüner Veltliner Im Weingebirge Smaragd. Both are decent, but which do you feel more drawn to?

I've tasted a small army of wines with quirky names and I'll be honest, I fully expected a lot of them to be ropey old dross. But some were reasonable. In fact, I found some absolute crackers.

Novelty names are harmless enough, but don't be lulled into a marketing gimmick. And wouldn't it be splendid if more wine labels were in plain English so we didn't need to rely on these tricks in the first place?

Pork, sausages, salamis and hams... there's a wine for every kind of piggy treat

I love pigs. I've been keeping them now for a couple of years with a couple of like-minded friends, and I can honestly say it's been a rewarding and cost effective way of feeding the family. It's also offered a uniquely wide window into the world of wine.

Presented with chops, hams, bacon, roasting joints and sausages, a wine loving pig fiend has a beautifully varied range of vino options to consider.

Let's start with the big daddy: roast pork. Now, roast pork is a curious meat, with a juicy, squidgy texture somewhere between red meat and white meat.

Big wines with chunky structure such as Cabernet Sauvignon and Shiraz tend to overwhelm the meat. But lighter styles of red can work – especially if you're emphasising your roast pork with a savoury gravy or chipolatas on the side.

Gamay is worth a try, and if you're looking for the best, Beaujolais cru wines are sensational – vivid, layered, bright and deft reds that'll appeal to lovers of fine Pinot Noir. You could also check out lighter Italian reds such as Barbera or Dolcetto – an elegantly fruity northern Italian beauty that has dark fruit flavours (think damson) with a tangy brightness. Grenache might also be a possibility for reds, and if you fancy a more fruity and forward version, look for it from Australia. Rosé is also an option.

But for me, with roast pork a white works best. You could try Viognier, but a late harvest Riesling cuts through the meat and embraces the apple sauce. Look for Spätlese on the label and try winemakers such as from the Mosel and Nahe regions. A late harvest German Riesling may not be everyone's cup of tea, but in my view they can be some of the world's finest wines, and as they're perceived to be out of fashion, they can offer supreme value as well.

Now then. Bangers. We all love 'em. They come in all sorts of shapes and sizes, from chipolatas to Cumberlands. Remember, the central theme is always going to be that meaty, savoury texture.

You can have a sip of white if you wish (go for one with a bit of richness and oak such as Viognier, Marsanne or Roussanne), but I reckon with a banger southern French reds are a winner. Fitou, Corbières and Minervois are all good shouts, but you could also try wines from Pic-St-Loup and beyond.

However, if your banger packs a meaty punch, the US is the place to trot to for wines made from the mighty grape called Zinfandel. It sounds like the name of a WWE wrestler, doesn't it?

I can see the catchphrases, the logo, the swishing red satin cape embossed with the words 'ZIN to WIN'. You may think I've gone bonkers describing a wine like this, but Zinfandel is a powerfully flavoured red with a dash of spice and depth. It's a bit like Grenache after a protein shake and a steroid injection.

Of course, sausages are often imbued with a dose of very dominant flavours, as in Spanish chorizo, which is like a meaty depth-charge enforced with garlic, smoked paprika and salt. If you're deploying chorizo in a stew or cassoulet, then I'd opt for a local wine such as a Tempranillo from Ribera del Duero or Rioja - Crianza if it's a weeknight in, or Reserva if it's a more special meal.

And what about salamis and charcuterie? Cabernet Franc from the Loire can be glorious with peppery cured meats, while Dolcetto works as a general choice. But if we're talking jamón ibérico – cured Spanish ham – you have to get your chops around some Spanish Fino, which is widely available for under a tenner.

They go together sensationally well thanks to the salty-briny affiliation. Meanwhile, if you're going for Italian Parma ham with melon balls, you could switch tack entirely and select a glass of Prosecco to contrast with the texture and pick up on the fruit.

You can try matching hams with dry whites – some swear by Chablis. But if I'm tucking into a simple ham sandwich with a smear of mustard, or a snack of honey roast ham, I'm honestly a fan of a decent English cider to complement the snack – especially if the ham is from my own hogs.

Piggylicious!

Everyday tipples to brighten up even the most autumnal weeknights

There a number of ways to spice up your everyday drinking. The first is to keep a few different bottles on the go so you can mix and match with your food, mood and budget.

Once you've opened a bottle, a pump with a rubber stopper will keep the contents fine for a few days. (If you want maximum shelf life, get yourself a can of wine preserver; it protects your wine with a blanket of magical gas that can keep it for up to a week or more.)

I love having at least three bottles chugging along for weeknight tippling, and I always have a bottle of bubbly in the fridge. You don't have to break the bank. A bottle of good value cava or Prosecco can be a welcome treat at the end of a tough day, and you can pick up a wide range of champagne stoppers to ensure brisk bubbles every time you re-open the bottle.

So, lesson number one, don't get stuck drinking the same old wine week in week out. Branch out, experiment and your weeknights will be more colourful. But what should you be buying?

For me, value is paramount. Chile has long been a bargain hunter's paradise, but the word on the grapevine is that France, which has recently received quite a kicking from the UK wine consumer, is picking up steam.

The labelling on French wines can be confusing since it is often by place rather than grape variety. But there are some reliable brands out there that you should be looking to buy.

And I'd also suggest looking to supermarket own label offerings from France: they all have some decent kit if it's bargains you're after.

I've long been a fan of Sicily for value. If you haven't already discovered the delights of local Italian whites such as Fiano and reds such as Nero d'Avola, they make a superb addition to your weeknight arsenal. These are fun and fruity wines that can match with a wide range of cooking.

You could, of course, look further afield – taste something a bit edgy and perhaps save a few pennies at the same time. Hungary is a fantastic place to look for good value white wines – and I've been tasting some good value reds from Spain, including Rioja Joven. I've also tried one or two cheeky reds from South Africa.

When you're getting wine for everyday drinking, it might be worth buying a case of six or 12 to save money – and take advantage of free delivery, with someone else doing the heavy lifting. I'm a big fan of ordering wine online.

Lastly, in addition to having a few good value bottles on the go, I'd urge you to keep a top quality bottle nearby, just in case you feel like something special. A great white, a romping red or an exquisite champagne can go a long way to making weeknights more fun.

I'm often asked when to drink a special bottle – perhaps one that's been given as a gift or that's been laying down for a long time. My advice is to make the wine the occasion. If you save it for an anniversary or birthday and the wine isn't what you were expecting, there's a far greater risk of disappointment than if you crack it open on a Tuesday night with your pork chops.

Trust me, even everyday drinking can taste great.

Trick or treat? How to hunt down a scarily good wine for Halloween

In the Smith household, Halloween that usually means getting together with other families for a full-on autumnal knees-up.

While the kids are scurrying about in their costumes, the adults can settle in for a good chinwag around some plates of nibbles and bottles of wine.

But what are the best wines for Halloween? Well, they could be ones that pair well with pumpkin dishes, but I reckon they're more likely to be wines that are in some way enthralling, surprising and a bit quirky. They're wines that befit the spooky sense of anticipation – that are great for a party but have that unexpected element.

With the leaves outside glowing orange, amber, yellow and scarlet, I love sipping richly flavoured whites, as a last hurrah before winter descends and hearty reds take over as the mainstay of my wine o'clock moments. Viognier is a brilliant grape variety to enjoy around now, with its rich peachy and apricot flavours. It can take a bit of spice in your food and works a treat with nibbles.

Its heartland is in France's Rhône valley, but there's plenty of outstanding Viognier to be found elsewhere in the world, from Australia to South Africa and beyond. Chile, for instance, is producing some very interesting Viognier, with invigorating freshness as well as rich fruit flavours.

Call me bonkers, but I also love to crack open a bottle of rosé around

Halloween. With autumn berries all the rage, it has a suitably festive colour, and it's the kind of wine that's versatile with food and also fun to serve at a party.

These days rosé comes in all shapes and sizes, from hearty, butch beauties that are so full of colour they're practically red wine through to delicate salmon pink pale examples that are so pale as to be almost water white.

You can of course age rosé champagne and some French rosés from Tavel, but generally it's a wine to drink young. For me it's all about fresh berry flavours, and I love to offer rosé to guests at my Halloween parties.

Rosé bubbly is also a good shout, from champagne to English sparkling wine to cava. Spanish cava in general is good value, and although it's created from local Spanish grapes, it's made with the same 'traditional method' used to make French champagne. It's perfect for your Halloween fiesta and lends itself very easily to cocktails.

As the harvest comes in and we ramp up to October 31, it's the time of year when the last fruits are hanging on the trees and the late harvest wines are beginning to take shape. I love late harvest sweet wines and still feel they're hugely underrated here in Britain. With a pudding they can be sublime – just make sure your dessert wine is sweeter than your pud.

But I'm also a big fan of serving sweet wine at the start of an evening, well chilled in small glasses and sometimes accompanied by one or two carefully chosen snacks. It may seem like a scary choice, but Halloween is the perfect time to try something a little quirky.

If you find sweet pudding wines too rich and cloying, have a sip of Moscato d'Asti from Italy – it's like grapey, sweet, frothy sherbet and is a fun, informal style of drink. It's also a winning match for dishes with dried fruit, from fruitcake to mince pies. Try it – you'll never find a wine that tastes more like freshly picked sweet white grapes.

Halloween offers the chance to break out, to behave as you wouldn't normally do. So don't go out and bully your neighbours for sweets and treats dressed up as a ghoul – instead, stock up on some tantalising new wines and take your taste buds on a tour.

It'll be more rewarding than rampaging on the streets, and if you invite your friends and neighbours over to explore the frontier of flavour with you, you can make Halloween the start of a new campaign – to take the fear out of tasting new wines.

What wines should you drink on Bonfire Night?

A wine for bonfire night has got to be smoky or spicy. Something to match with the fireworks, the scent of roasting chestnuts and the crackle of sparklers fizzing in the cold night breeze.

My home town of Lewes hosts an incredible bonfire night with a superb array of parades, fireworks and incendiary devices igniting the evening. The wines to match have got to be just as sensational.

The temptation on Bonfire Night is to stick to mulled wine, which is fine. I have two tips if you are making a mulled pot: firstly, warm it, don't boil it (you'll lose the booze) and, secondly, use port instead of brandy to boost the flavour and richness more seamlessly.

Now then, as far as wine goes, you may think that only reds can impart that smoky, spicy edge that fits with fireworks – but think again. Plenty of white wine has a smoky edge – Pouilly-Fumé from France is probably the most famous, made from 100 per cent Sauvignon Blanc.

But you can find it too in Riesling, such as those from Kamptal in Austria , where they make an exceptionally sexy, snappy, fragrant white.

You can also find quite funky smoky notes in certain southern French whites such as local blends from the Roussillon region.

Viognier, too, is a white that can sometimes offer a hint of gingery spice along with its trademark apricot-like flavours. Austrian Grüner Veltliner is a white that sometimes smells quite peppery, and Gewürztraminer is another white grape that has a world of spice about it often smelling and tasting similar to rose Turkish Delight.

You can find it in Alsace, Germany, Italy, Chile and further afield, but wherever it comes from it's usually a full-on fragrant tipple.

I've even tasted some examples of Sauvignon Blanc that smell and taste overwhelmingly – wait for it – of green bell peppers. I know it sounds strange but I've found a fair few of these uniquely pungent wines from Chile.

But it's not just grape varieties that can make a wine seem smoky and spicy. Oak can sometimes give a white a hint of toastiness as barrels are often toasted by lightly charring the inside to the specification of the winery, ranging from light toasty aromas to full-on smoky richness. Think of oak barrels as like a spice rack, which has a similar effect to marinating.

The range of flavours in oak is huge depending on where the oak comes from and how much it is toasted. The newer the oak, the greater impact on flavour – some winemakers prefer to use oak that has already held wine (known as first or second fill, depending on how many previous wines it's held) to obtain a more restrained result.

But, the touch-paper is truly lit with the widest range of spank and spice found in your red vino. Shiraz has got to be the first port of call and whether it's described as Shiraz or Syrah on the label, the chance of getting a smoky dimension to your wine is very high indeed.

For me, the magic of Shiraz is when it seems to be infused with a charry meatiness that no other grape variety can mimic. It's sublime, rich and deeply satisfying. If you like Shiraz, you should definitely be drinking Carmenère from Chile with its peppery spice, deep dark flavours and chocolatey richness. Grenache too can have a white peppery scent to it – you can find it in Spain labelled as Garnacha.

Grenache is the leading grape variety in Châteauneuf-du-Pape with its spicy power, and it's also part of the blend for red wines from Rioja that sometimes have a smoky niff. And if you're after smoke, the granddaddy of all the reds is South African Pinotage. It's a wine that people tend to love or hate with its dark smoky layers.

But if smoky wine isn't your thing, you could always stick to the mulled stuff – just don't boil it and to guarantee some fireworks, chuck in a hefty shot of port!

Settling down to a delicious feast? These wines will add the most to your Sunday roast

Ah, the roast: of all dishes the world over, this is the one we Brits have nailed. Whether it's cooked by your husband, mum, personal chef or granny, a roast is the muscular power potion that refuels us at the weekend so we can conquer the working week with the might of Bryn Terfel singing his face off.

So, big flavour, butch texture – surely a roast calls for the maximum hoof in your vino? Think again.

First of all, every roast is different. Roast beef is quite unlike roast cod, and while slow roasting can soften a dish to tenderness, faster cooking yields a more richly textured dish usually involving some crispy, crunchy action.

You've also got to consider the accompaniments. Horseradish is a wine killer, cranberry sauce boosts sweetness, mushrooms create a savoury richness and onions can add a caramelised edge. But whatever the specifics, the roast is a kingly dish, and selecting the perfect wine is essential to give it the royal treatment.

Let's start with game. You can divide game into dark game, such as venison and boar, and lighter game, including birds such as pheasant and grouse. For the latter, Pinot Noir is a safe bet, but if you're serving your roast with a creamy sauce or a fruity accompaniment, Pinot Gris from Alsace can provide the right texture and flavour. Where duck is concerned, Syrah from the northern Rhône is a winner, and pigeon, with its savoury touch, is a treat with Rioja.

Turning to darker game, venison is a lean, robust meat that demands some strength in your vino. Mourvèdre can work, as can Malbec – both are grapes you can find in south-west France. There are some who swear by the uniquely savoury tang of South African Pinotage.

And if it's boar on the menu, Fitou, Corbières and Minervois are traditional matches, but you could also try the firepower of some northern Italian reds with grape varieties such as Nebbiolo, or Spanish beauties such as Tempranillo from Ribera del Duero – a style that will appeal to fans of Rioja.

Speaking of which, Rioja Reserva and roast lamb is a match made in heaven. Red Bordeaux also works with lamb, as does Cabernet Sauvignon from elsewhere, but there's something magical about the sweet juiciness of lamb matched with a rocking Rioja – even if you're just having a simple dish of lamb chops with a Crianza.

Chicken offers a choice between red or white wine depending on the dish. Chicken with a meaty stuffing calls for a red, but a more fruity stuffing demands white wine. I always match coq au vin with the same colour of wine that's in the dish.

Reds to consider with chicken are lighter styles such as Gamay (the grape behind Beaujolais) and Pinot Noir. But if you're roasting your chicken with spicy flavours, have a look at South African Chenin Blanc.

Pork is another roast that can be matched with reds or whites – try the same low tannin reds as with chicken, and German Riesling (Spätlese) with apple sauce-enhanced pork roasts.

But perhaps the ultimate roast for a Brit is beef. Nothing beats a triumphant hit of roast beef with all the trimmings, and the received wisdom is that you should pair it with the best wine possible. Luckily, however, you don't need to break the bank – there are some amazing Argentinian Malbecs to partner roast beef for under a tenner.

Alternatively, you could go for a fine Bordeaux, a scrumptious Rioja Gran Reserva, an amazing Shiraz or Syrah such as Hermitage or Côte-Rôtie, or a stonking red from Spain's Priorat region. Beef is savoury, deep and rich, and as long as you choose a matching red with class and a decent whack of flavour, you'll be laughing. Roast on!

All the leaves are brown and the sky is grey... it's time to go California dreaming

I am surprised how many people I meet who declare they despise Californian wines. It's surprising for two reasons – firstly because of the huge output of big brands.

The second reason is that there are some excellent boutique wines from California – after all, this is the place that achieved a shock defeat over classic French wines in the blind tasting 'judgement of Paris' in 1976.

California is massive and there are many American viticultural areas, known as AVAs, within it, each with a slightly different approach to its wines. Napa Valley is perhaps the most famous but there are many more, such as Sonoma and Mendocino. There are also smaller AVAs such as the cooler Russian River Valley, which has a growing reputation for Pinot Noir. While I realise that poring over a map with a glass of wine isn't everyone's idea of a gripping night in, if you investigate the place your wine comes from it can go some way to explaining its characteristics.

There are several different grape varieties found across California to look out for.

For whites, Chardonnay rules the roost, but you can also find a few examples of Sauvignon Blanc, which is sometimes oaked and labelled 'Fumé' – a unique white with a smoky zing. I've seen a bit of Pinot Grigio around – but for a really thrilling Pinot Grigio I'd prefer to set my sights on bottles from northern Italy.

Rosé is big business too, with sweeter styles of 'blush' remaining popular, but where California really shines is with its reds. Cabernet Sauvignon can be outstanding and you can also find decent Syrah, some interesting Pinot Noir and some fascinating plantings of southern French grapes such as Mourvèdre, Grenache, Syrah and Counoise.

But the big bad grape that California has claimed for itself and pumps out with great exuberance is hearty red Zinfandel.

The best examples have liveliness and structure with fine drying tannin and rich oak that shouts for a hearty meal to accompany it – or you could age them for another decade to unlock their more savoury secrets.

On the organic side of wine production, California has some impressive credentials.

I guess that's where I really find the pedal meets the metal in California, with smaller wineries that are producing truly unique and expressive wines, whether it's iconic brands or smaller, boutique wineries.

It's wines like these that make me want to pick up my laptop, stride to the airport and get on a plane for LA. Or you could save your cash and splash a fraction of the cost of a plane ticket on a top wine – no passport required. Check in!

Those inventive chaps in Australia put
some wicked spin on classic wines.
It's not just cricket...

If you reckon Oz is only good for beefy reds and oaky Chardonnay,
think again. Like the cricket team, the Aussie winemaking fraternity
are inventive, comprise talent from distinctive regions and are prepared
to take risks to get the right result.

Oz produces wines of all shapes and sizes, from bright mineral-pure
whites right through to fizz, rosé, reds and luscious sticky pudding
wines.

In many ways, it was Aussie wine that helped me start out on my
journey into wine. The labels on the bottles conveyed information in
plain English and the wines stood out for their unstuffy sense of fun.

With whites you've got everything from Viognier to Riesling.
Semillon is a grape variety that performs brilliantly in the Hunter
valley. I have also been totally thrilled by a shrill, crisp white
Vermentino, a grape found more often in Sardinia.

Reds, too, offer a good selection, ranging from gutsy Shiraz and
rich Cabernet Sauvignon to more deft styles such as Pinot Noir.
With all these grape varieties at their fingertips, Australian winemakers are also producing a range of unique blends – sometimes with
unlikely combinations.

The signature Australian red blend is Shiraz-Cabernet, but there
are traditional Bordeaux style blends.

And it doesn't stop there.

Aussie know-how extends to making decent fizz, too. Meanwhile, sweet wines offer superb value and some top quality creations – one for your Christmas planning, as it pairs with mince pies, Christmas cake and Christmas pudding.

Talented winemakers abound in Oz, but creativity and knowledge would be nothing without the right soil and climate, and although the Australian wine scene has been knocked of late, it's bouncing back with a more regional focus. Look to Clare valley for Riesling, Coonawarra for Cabernet, Barossa for Shiraz, Victoria for Pinot Noir and Margaret River for boutique finesse.

And don't be afraid of the C-word (Chardonnay) – there are some superb and deftly oaked beauties out there.

Inject some derring-do into your wine choices by venturing off the beaten track and into the unknown

Choosing a wine you've never heard of may sound like folly, but sometimes if you peer beyond the safety of your regular purchase, you can not only save money but also find a wine that's totally delicious.

Take Hungary. It's a classic example of a place that makes decent wine but with names that are hard to pronounce; witness the excellent Cserszegi variety – a floral white that's usually a steal.

Or how about Greece? If you're a fan of bone dry whites with shrill acidity, such as Chablis, have you thought of getting your chops around an Assyrtiko?

Too often we Brits are lured by promotions or the safe choice with our vino; let's seize this chance together to try some wines with real personality – and save ourselves some cash.

One of the things I'm in favour of is wine being spoken about in terms we can understand.

I think the popularity of Aussie wine, which got a lot of people started on vino, is partly down to the labelling – in plain English, using everyday language and with a couple of decent nuggets of info. But if we stick to wine labels we know and understand, then our spectrum of pleasure is curtailed.

There are good reasons to take risks and sample the fruits of lesser known regions and places. You could be pleasantly surprised – for example, try Japanese wine made from the Koshu variety – it's a white with a delicate floral edge and great purity that reminds me of some of the finest Italian whites.

Whether you're a wine fan, a foodie or just someone who likes a drop of vino, it's wines such as this that'll keep you on your toes, engaging with new frontiers and the ever-changing map of wine production.

I've tasted long forgotten favourites from Germany as well as new wines from China, India ... and have you tasted Canadian wine? Some outstanding stuff is out there.

Of course, part of the problem might be that we don't understand what the wine label means, or indeed which bit of it refers to the grape variety. Have you ever heard of Rotgipfler? It's a white grape with amazing potential from Austria, featuring appley flavours with a subtle gingery spice.

Irsai Oliver? It's a Hungarian grape with very floral orangey touches, an exotic and often competitively priced white that works brilliantly with aromatic food flavours.

The best way to learn about wine is to taste it, so if you have a sure bet bottle in your basket, supplement it now and again with a new wine. If you like it, experiment with other wines from the place it came from; if not, try again – remembering that what you don't like in a wine is as important as what you do.

You should quickly figure out if you're a fan of spicy or oaky wine, crisp wine or mellow, fragrant styles.

And my best piece of advice is to ask questions – don't be afraid to explain what you're after.

There's one sure fire way to warm yourself up in winter: dive into the heady world of whisky

Whisky is powerful, enlivening and outrageous – I think of it as the drink of the gods. In the world of spirits, the range of whisky on offer is spectacular and tantalising.

You can divide whisky into several categories but the two big ones are single malts and blends. A single malt is the equivalent of fine wine, made in one distillery and not blended with any other whiskies. Blends are made from malt and grain spirit and tend to be less pricey than single malts.

Both have their place, but before you choose, it's helpful to know a bit about where whisky comes from.

Let's start with Japan. Yes, Japan. Japanese whisky is a relative newcomer but quality has been rising fast in recent years – and though it's hard to characterise an entire nation's output, Japanese whisky tends to have an appealing mellow character. It's been winning impressive awards and is without doubt here to stay.

Irish whiskey (note the spelling difference) is massively popular and is aged for around three years or more, giving it a softness that works superbly as a blending drink.

You can also find Irish single malts which are aged for longer, giving greater depth of flavour.

Wales too is making impressive whisky, and there's even a distillery in Norfolk, England.

Over in the US, bourbon is made mainly from corn grain and has a rounded sweetness thanks to developing the flavours in oak barrels.

But the granddaddy of whisky is, of course, Scotland. I spent four delicious years living in Edinburgh and remember perching myself in Kay's Bar on Jamaica Street week after week, steadily working my way through the whiskies to gain a deeper understanding of why they taste the way they do.

Much is down to the place. Speyside produces a very pure, thrilling spirit; the Highland whiskies can be floral and spicy or even a bit salty nearer the coast; Lowlands are approachable with an easygoing sweetness. You can explore Campbeltown and the Islands too.

But I urge you to sample the delights of Islay (you say it 'Eye-la'). Islay whisky has a rich smoky touch to it and eight distilleries to choose from. It's the most full-on style and you could liken it to Shiraz in the wine world – bold flavours, smoky and utterly more-ish.

The mighty question of how to drink whisky is one that can spark very heated discussions. Personally I find that ice tends to mute the flavours of a single malt and I go for a splash of water to bring out the flavours. But with all the types of whisky, how you take it becomes as personal as polishing your imaginary sports car.

Don't be afraid of whisky. To me, the flavour is sensational and all of us should be forced to salute every Scot out of respect for the genius bestowed on the world.

Sherry isn't just for granny – in fact, there's no cooler way to kick off the festive season

Sherry is the drink we Brits associate with the festive season, and working my way through the various bottles, I can see why: the warming range of flavours seems beautifully suited to keeping snug.

Yet sherry comes from Spain's hot south, and I can't help thinking we're missing a trick by not enjoying this delicious drink all year round. You may think it's strictly for grannies, but I'm no granny and I love the stuff.

Many chefs are fans – including Heston Blumenthal – and it's well worth rediscovering the treasures on offer.

In Spain, Fino sherry fuels the start of a night out for young and old alike, and at the Easter-time ferias in Seville and Jerez, the entire party is powered by sherry.

The most important thing to understand about the fortified favourite is that it's not all brown and sweet. To think so is akin to believing all ballroom dancers are like Ann Widdecombe.

As with dancing, there's a world of different styles of sherry to sample and match with the food you're eating or the mood you're in.

The lightest and brightest style of sherry is Manzanilla, closely followed by Fino. These two have a glorious nutty niff, but when sipped manage to be refreshing and savoury at the same time.

Tangy and bright, these are the drinks to inject some sparkle into your evening. If you're partial to a Dirty Dry Martini, with a salty, olive twist, you need to get your chops round Manzanilla or Fino. Serve them cold in small glasses with nibbles (jamón ibérico works a treat) and your palate will instantly reach cruising altitude. They'll give your taste buds a polish in preparation for the feast ahead.

Manzanilla is widely available for under a tenner and is the perfect introduction to sherry. Grab it and serve it well chilled with a few olives, hunks of Manchego cheese and jamón ibérico to add a Spanish touch to your festive celebrations. Magnificent tangy bright kit.

Then you can ratchet up the richness. Amontillado sherry tends to be dry and nutty, and Palo Cortado can be aged and highly savoury, but for me, the really wondrous diversity of sherry is shown off by Oloroso.

Oloroso means 'fragrant', and it's an amazing style of sherry that comes both dry and sweet.

It's a brilliant bet with hard cheese, meaty snacks or just as a glass of amazing aged wine to savour with a good book... or better yet, a cuddle. Oloroso can also be sweetened, which makes for an amazing match with Christmas cake, mince pies and other festive foods – think dried fruit and spice; it's all the flavours of Christmas in a single sip.

The sweetest of all sherries is Pedro Ximénez, or PX for short. It's like a dark, thick, rich syrup of dates and figs. It's fruity and fantastic and can work with Christmas pudding – or just pour it over a scoop of vanilla ice cream for an indulgent treat.

The world of sherry is a bit like a choir of carol singers, with voices ranging from bright and shrill right through to deep and rich. Quite apart from the wealth of flavours and styles on offer, sherry remains one of the true bargains of the wine world. You can pick up wines aged and tended for 30 years or more for the price of two tickets to the cinema. Take a tip from the great grannies out there and grab a bottle of the good stuff.